Where The Trail Meets The Heart

A Midlife Story of Strength & Healing

Linda A. Banks

Published by Linda A. Banks Press
ISBN (Paperback): 979-8-9945838-0-7
Cover design by Marissa Banks

Dedication

For my father,
the man who chose us when the world didn't expect it. You were my first lesson in what real love looks like, and I think of you far more often than words can hold.

For my husband, Darryl,
thank you for being steady when I wasn't. Thank you for staying close through the good parts and the hard ones, and for believing in me when my confidence went missing.

For my daughters, Marissa and Emmie,
watching you become who you are has been one of the great gifts of my life. I hope what you hear in these pages isn't "perfect," but real, and that it reminds you that you can keep trying and still be whole.

For my friends, and my running-and-walking family,
thank you for showing up. For the laughs, the long talks, the quiet support, and the miles we didn't do alone.

And for every woman who sees herself here,
if you've been holding it together for everyone else, or rebuilding in ways nobody sees, I wrote this for you too. I hope you find something true here, and the nudge you need to take the next step.

With love,

Linda

A Note on Trail Truths

Trail Truths appear at the start of every chapter. They aren't meant to be perfect slogans or polished advice. They're the kind of thoughts that come after enough miles, laughter, tears, and time spent walking beside people you love.

I've spent thousands of hours on trails with dear friends in what we half-jokingly call "therapy sessions." Somewhere between the switchbacks and the quiet, we talk about everything: grief, marriage, motherhood, aging, fear, courage, and the stubborn hope that keeps coming back. These Trail Truths are what surfaced from those miles and those conversations.

Some came straight from me. Some were sparked by the people who've walked with me. Most are a blend, less a quote and more a distillation. Either way, they're offered here the same way they were first spoken, simply, honestly, and with love.

Table of Contents

Introduction

I didn't set out to write a book about midlife. I wrote it because I kept meeting women who were doing a lot, carrying a lot, and quietly shrinking anyway. I know that pattern because I lived it.

Somewhere along the way, I became the woman who could hold everything together and still feel like I wasn't doing enough. I could remember everyone else's needs and forget my own. I could show up for other people while my own life got put on hold so long it started to feel normal.

I'm not writing this as someone who has it all figured out. I don't feel more capable than most women my age. I still wrestle with self-belief. The difference is that I started doing hard things anyway, and that changed me.

Running was my doorway, even though I never would have picked myself as "a runner." When I finished my first 5K, people cheered. It sounds small, but it hit me in a way I didn't expect. It was the first time I remember being celebrated for being strong in my own body, and I can still hear that crowd. Something in me woke up and thought, oh, there you are.

Then ultramarathons showed up. And yes, four marathons back-to-back is not a reasonable hobby. Nobody finishes a marathon and casually decides to do it three more times. But ultrarunning taught me something I didn't expect. You break the impossible into steps, you keep showing up, and somehow it becomes doable. That lesson followed me off the trail and into the rest of my life.

Caregiving did too, in a different way. It was its own kind of ultra, and it asked more of me than running ever did. With running, at least you know the distance and the course. Caregiving does not hand you a map. You don't get to know how long it will last or what it will take, and the emotional toll is heavy in a way people understand only after they have lived it. Time is the thing that gave me my smile back. I did not believe that would happen while I was in the middle of it.

The point of this book isn't to turn you into a runner - it's to remind you that your life can expand in any direction you choose. Whether your doorway is hiking, travel, yoga, writing, or simply saying yes to something you've wanted for years, what matters most is that you stop treating your own life like it comes last.

Along the way, I'm going to give you short reflection pauses, like a bench on the trail. You can use them or skip them. You can write in the margins, cry, laugh, or stare at the wall for a minute and call it productive. I'm here to share what helped me and what didn't.

If you've been wondering whether you missed your moment, I want to offer a different question.

What if it is not too late, and you're just scared to believe that?

Your story is still unfolding. Because courage does not belong only to the young. And because the life ahead of you is still worthy of curiosity, movement, wonder, healing, and joy, if you're willing to whisper, even a little shakily:

Why not me?

CHAPTER 1
Why Not You?

Trail Truth: If you're waiting to feel confident first, you'll be waiting a long time.

Telling my story still feels a little odd. I've spent most of my life cheering from the sidelines, not stepping into the middle of the field and talking about myself.

Being steady has always felt natural to me. People counted on me, and I liked being that person.

For years, Darryl traveled a lot for work, and I ran the home front. Calendars, carpools, volunteering, and all the day-to-day stuff that keeps a family moving. The girls were cared for, and the wheels stayed on. It was behind-the-scenes work, and I took pride in it. It held our family together.

I loved those years. I wanted that life, and I was good at it. I also know that not everyone gets that option, and I've never taken it for granted. The tricky part came later, when taking care of everyone stayed set to "on" even after the girls didn't need me in the same way.

Somewhere along the way, I stopped feeling like myself.

It happened slowly, the way it often does when you're busy and capable and used to handling life. I kept telling myself I would do something for me later. I kept putting my needs behind whatever felt more urgent that day. After a while, that became normal.

From the outside, everything looked fine, even good. Inside, I felt oddly disconnected from my own life, like I was present for it but not fully inside it. I didn't have a neat explanation, and I didn't talk about it much, because it felt ungrateful to admit.

The question still showed up.

Where did I go?

If you've ever loved your life and still felt a little lost inside it, I hear you. Running started as a small attempt to feel like myself again. I wanted proof there was still a spark in me that belonged only to me.

What I didn't see coming was how far that spark would reach. I thought I was taking one small step for myself. I had no idea I was lighting a trail we'd all end up walking and running together.

When Darryl noticed it, he laced up his shoes too. He came back to something he loved and had set aside. The girls started running with us. Unlike me, they had a natural gift for it. They ran cross-country in middle school and high school, and our oldest ran in college. They still run to this day.

And my early "running" was a sight. I shuffled more than I ran. I questioned my life choices about every thirty seconds. I avoided eye contact with the neighbors because nobody needed to witness that situation.

Underneath the awkwardness, something in me kept insisting I try again. I showed up anyway.

The miles got longer and the mornings got earlier. Some runs made me want to quit halfway through. Some turned into full-on negotiations. A few had me wondering what I was trying to prove, and who I thought I was proving it to.

We trained through the god-awful North Carolina summer, hot, humid, relentless, plus plenty of rain showers for good measure.

That's why this story matters to me. Running was the start. The real work was turning back toward my own life and admitting I wanted to be in it, not just managing it.

Here's what surprised me. Wanting something for yourself can sit right alongside gratitude. You can love your life and still want more room to breathe inside it.

If you've ever had the thought, "Could I really do something like that," you don't have to answer it all at once. Start smaller. Start where you are. Take one step that belongs to you and see what changes.

If you're waiting for a sign that you're allowed, consider this one.

Reflection Pause

Where in my life have I underestimated myself?

____

____

____

What is something I once believed I could never do, yet eventually did?

____

____

____

What is one meaningful thing that scares me a little…probably because it matters?

____

____

____

When I whisper, "Why not me?" what shows up first: fear, hope, doubt, excitement?

____

____

____

If I trusted myself even a tiny bit more than I do today, what might I reach for?

____

____

____

CHAPTER 2
First Steps

Trail Truth: If you've been giving yourself away in small pieces, you're allowed to take some back.

Somewhere in my 40s, my body stopped bouncing back the way it used to. My metabolism shifted, everything else took priority, and I quietly stopped taking care of myself. Years of showing up for everyone else, managing, organizing, fixing, and planning had taken a toll.

Then suddenly the woman living in your own skin feels unfamiliar. My joints had opinions and my energy had limits. Learning to be kind to this newer version of myself took time.

Maybe you've been there too.

I kept coming back to the same thought: I wanted to come back to myself. So, I did the only thing I could think of.

I joined a local Couch to 5K training group. I joined because I needed a lifeline. I needed something that belonged to me, something not tied to a role or an expectation or a checklist. I wanted proof that it wasn't too late to feel alive again.

When I first started, I couldn't run a single block without my lungs and legs staging a full-scale protest. My body was genuinely confused about what I was asking it to do. I watched other people float forward while I was over there negotiating with myself. Just don't collapse and we'll call it a win.

Those early runs humbled me. I was bringing up the rear, even in a group of beginners. There were days I wanted to cry and times when I genuinely wondered what in the world I was doing there.

I stayed anyway.

Showing up became its own quiet kind of courage. I kept moving when I didn't feel confident, when my body protested, and my brain whispered this is embarrassing. Then slowly, something shifted. I stopped criticizing myself and started respecting the effort. Somewhere in the middle of all that huffing and shuffling, I felt something I hadn't felt in a long time. A small flicker of pride.

Our group had two coaches. One of them was warm and encouraging and genuinely invested in every single one of us. She celebrated the tiny wins, the awkward shuffles, the "I ran for sixty seconds without dying" moments. She made you feel like you mattered.

The other coach was more reserved. Not unkind, just less connected.

On our mock 5K practice day, that difference showed up clearly. I gave everything I had and still finished dead last. By the time I crossed the line, the other coach had stopped timing and gone inside. No clock, no results, no acknowledgment from her. Just me standing there with burning lungs, shaky legs, and a quiet sting I didn't quite know what to do with.

But the nurturing coach stayed. She looked me in the eye and told me she was proud of me. She reminded me that finishing at any pace mattered.

Still, that moment of being uncounted landed hard. It handed me a clarity I didn't expect: if someone else wasn't going to count me, then I was going to count myself. I needed to decide who I was going to be, someone who quit, or someone who kept going.

I chose to keep going.

So, when I lined up for my first official 5K, the Women's Race for the Cure, I was proud to be there. I was surrounded by women of every age and size. Some were fighting far bigger battles than me. Some fought for every step.

When I came down that final stretch and heard cheering, cheering for me, something in me cracked open. It was the first time in my life anyone had cheered for me simply for being strong in my own body. They weren't celebrating perfection or speed. They were celebrating heart.

Crossing that finish line was hard. It was hot and humid, and my legs were done with the whole thing. But standing there among these women who were doing something just for themselves felt like belonging.

I had finally found my people.

Reflection Pause

When was the last time I felt like I was starting from scratch?

____

____

____

When I begin something new, do I treat myself with grace or with pressure?

____

____

____

Where in my life am I "at the back of the pack," but still showing up anyway?

____

____

____

What do I need more of right now: discipline, compassion, or courage?

____

____

____

What tiny first step could I take toward something that matters to me?

____

____

____

CHAPTER 3
Standing at the Start Line of Something Bigger

Trail Truth: If it makes you nervous and excited, pay attention.

I didn't expect a 5K to do much more than leave me sweaty and sore. Instead, it flipped a switch.

Finishing that first 5K woke something up in me. Running stopped being "exercise." It became a way to build trust with myself again. Every mile reminded me there was still strength, courage, humor, stubbornness, and heart inside me, even in midlife, even while my body was changing, even with life still pulling at me from forty-seven different directions.

That's when a friend invited me into a half-marathon training group.

A half marathon. Thirteen point one miles. That alone felt like plenty to chew on. It sounded like something for women who seemed naturally athletic, confident, and capable. Definitely not women juggling hormones, stress, responsibility, doubts, and that little voice that says, are you sure this is a good idea?

I almost said no. I'd spent years telling myself to be reasonable, to accept slowing down, to stay within safe, manageable expectations. Doubt sounds practical when you've been listening to it that long.

But something inside me refused to shrink.

So, I said yes.

And that's how I found myself standing in a parking lot on a chilly Saturday morning for the Jeff Galloway Half and Full Marathon Training Program, at 42 years of age, wondering what in the world I had gotten myself into.

That first day felt like walking into school after the bell had already rung, when everyone seems to know where they're going except you.

I didn't even start on week one. I joined in week two, which meant their "easy Saturday run" was six miles. Six. The longest distance I had ever run in my life was three, and even that had felt like a miracle. So, when I heard we were about to double it, I was scared out of my mind.

I didn't know enough about running to know what happens when you can't run anymore. But I figured if I was going to fall apart, at least I'd be surrounded by people who could get help. And somehow, mile by mile, I did it. Once we started moving, something surprising happened. The miles didn't feel like punishment. They felt like air.

We talked. We laughed. And it turns out there's something incredibly honest about walking or running next to someone instead of sitting across from them. Walls come down and people open up. I learned how many women were quietly carrying so much: aging parents, loss, illness, complicated marriages, loneliness, child rearing concerns, menopause, changing bodies, fading confidence, grief, fear, and hope.

The group was coed, but I gravitated toward the women runners. The conversations went places that felt real, the kind of things you don't always say out loud in regular life. Out there on the road, nobody cared what you looked like, what you weighed, what you did for a living, or what your title was. There was no competition. We showed up, did the work, and pulled for each other.

And let me say this. Women are tougher than we give ourselves credit for.

The Jeff Galloway program gave me more than structure. It gave me people. Real, lifelong people. Some runners went on to run marathons in all 50 states. Some ran on all seven continents.

And then there was our core group of women who, to this day, still meet for dinner, still check in, and show up. My husband and I even traveled to Iceland this year and met up with two couples we met in that program over twenty years ago. That's the kind of community running gave me: people who stay.

That first six-mile run felt monumental. I had finished and still felt whole. I felt expanded instead of shrinking. For the first time in a long time, it felt like my body and my spirit were finally on the same team.

I liked training. Even when it was stupid hot and humid, at least I was suffering with friends. The miles went by faster when you had people beside you who could make you laugh and remind you why you showed up in the first place. Underneath all of that, one promise stayed steady: I'm not disappearing again.

Somewhere along the way, that original half-marathon goal got left in the dust. I was strongly encouraged to keep going and slide right into marathon training, and I didn't exactly fight it. After my first fourteen-mile training run, I came home satisfied and glowing, and Darryl took notice. He started to think there might be something to this Jeff Galloway walk-run approach after all. To be fair, he'd been a runner most of his life and had a natural ability I didn't have. He jumped back in, and suddenly we were doing it together.

Training changed how I saw myself. I wasn't building endurance for a race. I was building endurance for my life.

And I wasn't doing it alone. I was surrounded by people who laughed, sweated, struggled, encouraged, and stayed. Their courage pulled me forward right alongside my own.

Then race day came.

Richmond is known as "America's Friendliest Marathon," and it lives up to that name.

The course starts downtown, then turns onto Monument Avenue with those grand historic homes that make you feel like you've wandered back in time. It's beautiful in that old, stately way. Then the route winds through neighborhoods where people set out their own little aid stations like they're hosting a block party. Water, snacks, signs, music, and yes, for those so inclined, "shots of courage." I remember seeing them and thinking, this is either genius or a terrible idea. Possibly both.

The early miles feel almost fun. You've trained for months for this day, so there's something exciting about watching your plan come together. Rolling hills, friendly faces, that nervous energy where everyone is still smiling and feeling good. You cross the James River and for a while it feels like you might be the kind of person who runs marathons now. Like you do. No big deal.

Then mile 19 shows up.

Mile 19 has a hill you are in no mood for when it hits. Your legs are tired, your brain is bargaining, and suddenly the course asks you to climb. You do not rise to the occasion. You trudge and dig. You tell yourself whatever you must to keep moving.

After that, you head into the gritty industrial part of town. Those miles get quiet. A kind of focused quiet. I like to call it the dig-deep miles. Nobody's out there doing it for fun anymore. You're out there because you said you would be, and because some part of you refuses to quit.

And then, somehow, you make your way back toward downtown.

The energy builds again like the city is pulling you home. And then comes that glorious downhill finish where everyone gets to feel like a hero. The crowds are electric. People are cheering like they know you and have been waiting for your arrival.

There is truly nothing like finishing your first marathon.

Crossing that finish line didn't magically turn me into a new woman. It helped me finally meet the woman I had always been.

And yes, there was ugly crying. It was my first marathon. I earned every tear.

A marathon doesn't change you as much as it reveals you. It pulls forward grit, tenderness, stubborn hope, humor, resilience, and that refusal to quit. Honestly, women in midlife already have those things in abundance. We simply forget we do, because we're usually too busy holding everything together.

Standing there at the finish, exhausted, emotional, and feeling more alive than I had in years, one truth settled deeply into me. I had much more life to live.

Life felt like it had opened wider. Maybe this wasn't the peak or the last big thing.

Maybe it was just the start.

Reflection Pause

Where in my life have I surprised myself with strength I didn't expect?

___

___

___

What helped me keep going when quitting would've been easier?

___

___

___

Who has encouraged me when I doubted myself, and have I thanked them, or myself?

___

___

___

What dream feels "too big" right now, and why might it still be worth considering?

___

___

___

CHAPTER 4
When the Fire Catches

Trail Truth: The afterglow fades. The fire doesn't have to.

After my first marathon, I felt different in a way that's hard to explain without sounding cheesy, so I'll just say it plainly. I trusted myself more. I had trained for something hard, shown up anyway, and finished.
That mattered.

For a while, I rode that high. I'd be folding laundry or sitting at a red light and the memory would pop into my head like, oh yeah, I did that. The best part wasn't the medal or the bragging rights. It was the way it changed the way I talked to myself.

Then the question hit me.

Now what?

People skip over that part. You work toward a goal for months, you cross it off, and then you wake up the next morning with the same life waiting for you. Only now you know you're capable of more, and it's hard to go back to playing small.

Over the next few years, I ran more half marathons and more full marathons. Some races were pure fun, the kind where you laugh with friends and the miles go by without you noticing. Other races felt quieter and more personal, where running gave me something steady when life felt heavy. Either way, the same thought kept returning.

There's more in me than I've been using.

Running became a declaration of sorts. It reminded me I wasn't done, and it proved my dreams didn't come with an expiration date.

That's when ultrarunning started tapping me on the shoulder.

Darryl and his running buddies had wandered into the little-known world of ultrarunning, and I watched it pull him in. He'd come home exhausted, sore, dusty, scraped up, and somehow deeply satisfied. He talked about solitude and struggle, about long stretches of trail where your brain gets loud and your legs get stubborn, about finishing with a kind of pride that had nothing to do with attention.

Every time he told another story, I found myself leaning in.
The word "ultra" sounded like it belonged to another universe. These races were nothing like the city marathons I was used to. Ultras lived on trails, back roads, and long quiet stretches of nature. It was hours of effort and people making one decision after another to keep moving forward.

Could I do something like that?

Before I ever attempted one myself, I stood on the sidelines of Darryl's first 100-miler, and it rattled me more than I expected. The distance sounded impossible. The hours felt unreal. My brain went straight to the practical worries.

Can a person really endure this? What if something goes wrong?

I spent a lot of that race at headquarters, watching runners come and go in every imaginable state of exhaustion and determination. It was intense. It was also oddly grounding, because these weren't superheroes. They were regular people in all shapes, sizes, and ages.

At some point, a woman with a mischievous grin and a spark in her eyes noticed me hovering. I probably looked curious and overwhelmed, maybe a little starstruck, and unsure what to do with myself. She waved me over like, if you're here, you may as well be useful.

That woman was Sally Squier.

Sally started running ultras in the era when people warned her, completely seriously, that all that running would make her "lady junk" fall out. She tells it now with that classic Sally mix of humor and shrug, like: well, that didn't happen. What did happen is she found her strength and kept it.

At the time, I knew nothing about her. I had no idea how many races she'd finished or what her background was. What I did know was that she had this mix of toughness and joy that made you feel steadier just standing near her. She was calm in a place that felt chaotic to me. She moved like she knew what mattered and what didn't and didn't waste energy on anything else. Later I learned she'd finished more than a few hundred-milers. That explained a lot. She carried herself like someone who had already been to the dark places and knew the way back.

I nicknamed her "Sally Hard-as-Nails," because truly, that's who she is. Fierce. Kind. Hilarious. Sharp. No-nonsense. Full-hearted.

Standing beside her at that aid station, I got a front-row seat. Exhaustion meeting compassion. Toughness meeting humor. Fear showing up and people moving through it anyway. Sally didn't baby anyone, but she also didn't dismiss what they were feeling. She met them where they were, told the truth, handed them what they needed, and helped them keep moving.

At one point a runner came in looking wrecked, the kind of wrecked that makes you wonder if they're done. Sally looked them right in the eye, flashed that signature grin, and said:

"If the bone ain't showing, you keep on going."

She could tell the difference between pain and danger. Between discomfort and real trouble. Between "I'm over this" and "I actually need help."

Somewhere in those long hours beside Sally, the fear in me loosened its grip. The intimidation backed off. My respect grew, and my curiosity dug in and refused to leave.

This wasn't madness. This was strength and community, plain and simple, with no polishing.

Sally showed me, just by being who she is, that women are capable of far more than we're taught to believe. Age didn't limit her. Fear didn't run her life. She stood there as living proof that joy, humor, and backbone don't expire.

She became a quiet hero in my life, one of those women who clears space without even trying. She was part of the reason I stopped standing on the edge of that world and started imagining myself in it.

And somewhere in the middle of that loud, unforgettable race environment, the question I once thought was too bold to even say out loud finally formed, clear as day.

If she can, why not me too?

Reflection Pause

Where in my life have I gone farther than I ever thought I could?

____

____

____

What do I usually tell myself when something feels "too big," and is that voice protecting me or limiting me?

____

____

____

Who are the "Sallys" in my life, the women who inspire me simply by how they live?

____

____

____

When I think about aging, strength, and possibility, what beliefs am I ready to rewrite?

____

____

____

If I tried, what's the smallest first step I could take without scaring myself into quitting?

____

____

____

CHAPTER 5
Breathing Different Air

Trail Truth: This wasn't about applause. It was about answering my own questions.

By this point, I had been running for a few years and had finished several marathons. Still, I wanted more. Ultrarunning tugged at me in a curious way, like my brain was asking, how much more is in there? Eventually I decided to find out.

I started with what people jokingly call the "shallow end" of ultras: a 50K. An ultramarathon is anything beyond 26.2 miles, and 50K is the most recognized first ultra distance. Thirty-one miles and change.

The New River 50K in Galax, Virginia felt like the right place to start. It was a steady, relatively flat gravel path winding along scenery that kept showing up at exactly the right time to distract you from the fact that you're running thirty-one miles. The river stayed alongside the course for long stretches, and I loved that.

Race day was wonderfully simple. Blue sky, trees, gravel, breath, rhythm. Darryl ran beside me the entire way and having him there mattered. He's steady company. When I'm chatty, he plays along. When I get quiet, he doesn't try to fill the space.

The weather was perfect; the kind of day built for running. I was excited to dip my toes into ultra territory and see what happened once I passed 26.2. I kept wondering, how is that going to feel? The course was flat, which meant I could settle into a steady rhythm and stay consistent. The miles just kept ticking off, one after another, and it felt almost suspiciously smooth.

Late in the race, I found myself leapfrogging with the same few women over and over. I'd pass them, they'd pass me, and it turned into this annoying little dance. Finally, Darryl looked at me, tired, amused, and absolutely done with the suspense, and said, "Linda, for the love of God, pass these women for once and for all. I am not watching them beat you to the finish."

I laughed and did exactly that.

Eventually the finish line came into view. When I crossed it, I felt tired, steady, emotional, and proud. The part I kept waiting on, the moment after 26.2 where everything was supposed to fall apart, never really showed up. I just kept moving. Mile after mile, I did what I came to do.

Afterward, standing there at the finish line taking it all in, I realized something simple. I liked that world. I liked the quiet, the steady effort, the way nobody cared what you looked like.

And somewhere in that, the curiosity turned into something more certain. I wasn't just wondering if I could do an ultra anymore. I knew I could.

Reflection Pause

Where in my life have I surprised myself recently, even in a small way?

____

____

____

Do I trust myself when something gets difficult, or do I doubt myself first?

____

____

____

What helps me stay when things become uncomfortable instead of immediately backing away?

____

____

____

How do I feel when I imagine myself doing something a little bigger than what feels "safe"?

____

____

____

Where do I sense possibility tugging at me right now, and what would one small "yes" look like?

____

____

____

CHAPTER 6
Umstead 50: Dipping a Toe in the Deep End

Trail Truth: Sometimes you don't need confidence. You just need to show up.

Thirty-one miles should probably be enough for any sane person. Somehow, it wasn't enough for me. That's the thing about ultrarunning, and about midlife too. Once you finally see your own strength, curiosity kicks in.

So, I signed up for the fifty-mile option at the Umstead 100 Mile Endurance Run. It felt like stepping past the edge of what I knew, just to learn, grow, and see what else was possible.

I trained in early mornings and on long weekends. I learned the practical stuff that makes or breaks an ultra: what I could eat and drink for hours, what shoes and layers held up, and what could throw me off if I ignored it. Mostly, I learned how to work with the body I had, the one that had lived a full life and still showed up.

At forty-eight years old, I stood on the starting line. They play the national anthem, the gun goes off, and that's it. Off you go into the darkness before dawn.

Headlamps bobbed through the trees like a quiet little parade. Just breath, footsteps, nervous energy, and the steady awareness that you are about to be out here for a while.

Umstead is run in loops - four 12.5-mile circuits for the fifty-mile race, with two aid stations roughly six miles apart. It's equal parts comforting and brutal. Each loop brings a chance to refuel and regroup, but also a moment of choice: head back out or sit down and start convincing yourself you've done "enough."

The early miles passed calmly. I found myself running alone for stretches, which scared me at first. I felt in over my head. But I stayed disciplined, trusting my pace rather than getting swept up in the energy around me. Fifty miles rewards patience, not adrenaline. And I learned something: being alone didn't mean being lonely. Sticking to my plan, even when it felt uncertain, was exactly what I needed to do.

Being alone out there grounded me. It reminded me how rare it is to simply be with yourself without distraction or performance. No one setting your pace or defining your worth. Just your breath, your body, your stubborn heart, and the decision to keep going.

Of course, ultras have a way of weaving connection into the day whether you planned for it or not. I fell into step with other runners - strangers at first, not for long. You end up sharing the trail with fellow newbies and first timers as well as veterans, and everyone has their own "why." Unlike road marathons where the focus is on pace or chasing a PR, ultras have a different culture. The main goal is to finish. Nobody cared who was "fast." We cared about what it takes to keep moving when it would be far easier to stop.

Around mile thirty-seven and a half, I came into the aid station after my third loop, and there sat my dear friend Angela. She looked calm, unbothered, and spectacularly done. She had a burger in one hand, chocolate milk in the other, and the look of a woman completely at peace with her life choices. If there had been a recliner available, she would have claimed it and asked for a cozy blanket. She had also found a charming man to chat with, which did not hurt her willingness to stay parked.

To be fair, she made an excellent case. Thirty-seven and a half miles is wildly respectable.

The problem was, I know Angela and I know her heart. Her heart had not come for "pretty close."

So, I walked over with love wrapped in firmness and said, "No, ma'am. We did not come here for thirty-seven and a half miles."

She tried logic and humor. She waved that burger like Exhibit A. Deep down, though, she already knew she didn't want to quit. She just didn't want to walk back into the hard part alone.

I was so focused on getting her up and moving that I didn't even register what was happening with me. I was sweaty, damp, and the sun was starting to dip. I was about to head right back out in a wet sports bra, tempting fate.

That's when Sally appeared.

Sally Squier has a gift. One look at you and she knows exactly what you need. She doesn't mince words.

She took one look at me and said, "Get in there and change your sweaty sports bra. You're going to get hypothermia if you go back out like that." And let me tell you, when Sally tells you something like that, you do it.

That was Sally. Tough, caring, and practical in the way that keeps people safe. She knew the difference between being uncomfortable and being in danger, and she wasn't going to let me confuse the two.

So, bra changed and ready to go, I looked Angela in the eye and made my promise. "We're going to finish this together." Simple as that. Just two women saying, okay, fine. Let's go. And we did, because that's what women do. We drag each other back into courage when the other one forgets she has it.

And then, when I thought the day couldn't give me anything more, mile forty-four delivered something I will carry forever. Waiting for me, bright-eyed and practically gleaming, was my daughter Emmie, ready to run the last six miles with me to the finish.

She was a young middle schooler then, full of bounce and wonder, darting ahead, laughing, touching trees, absorbing everything. For six miles, I got to see the trail through her eyes - fresh, bright, full of possibility. And she got to see me doing something hard, something that mattered, something I chose.

Kids don't always understand what they're witnessing, but they feel it. Emmie may not have grasped ultrarunning or mileage math, but what mattered landed anyway: her mother refusing to shrink, effort and joy sharing space, proof that getting older doesn't mean disappearing.

Even if children don't grow up and say, *Mom, witnessing your endurance shaped my core belief system,* you can tell when something lands. They store evidence and remember how it felt. Whether we realize it or not, they are watching.

Angela and I crossed that finish line with Emmie between us - her fresh energy pulling us forward, my determination showing her what's possible, and Angela's refusal to quit, proving that we show up for each other no matter what. It was everything.

And then came one of those perfectly absurd, very-ultra, very-Umstead moments. Umstead isn't technically a "fifty-mile race." It's a hundred-mile race with a fifty-mile option. Which means that when you cross the line at fifty miles, proud and emotional and fully alive, the assistant race director looks at you and says, "Okay, you're officially dropping?"

He wasn't rude and he wasn't wrong. Technically, yes, I was dropping.

But in that surreal second, there was this ridiculous collision of truths. Was I dropping? Yes. Was I also triumphant? Also, yes. Did I just run fifty miles and deserve at least a small parade? Absolutely yes.

We laughed about it later, because even acknowledging the technical term, my heart knew the truth. I didn't feel like someone who quit. I felt like someone who had stepped more fully into her own life.

If anything, something deep inside me had stood up.

Crossing that finish line made something clear to me. Worth was already there. The finish simply made it easier to feel. It brought my resilience into focus, the kind that had been growing quietly for a long time.

Women over fifty carry big dreams in hearts that have already lived a whole lot of life. Age teaches courage in a way nothing else can.

If something inside you whispers, maybe me, maybe now, maybe it isn't too late, listen to it. Courage can look like showing up. It can look like accepting help. It can look like telling the truth about where you've been and choosing what comes next.

That day, another chapter of mine very clearly began.

Reflection Pause

Where in my life did I stop at "good enough," even though a part of me really wanted to keep going?

Who are the "Angelas" in my life, the people who make hard things lighter because we face them together?

When was the last time I surprised myself with what I could handle emotionally, physically, or spiritually?

Where do I feel quietly seen in my life, maybe by my kids, partner, friends, or someone I didn't expect?

What is one place in my life where curiosity is whispering, maybe me, maybe now, maybe it's not too late?

CHAPTER 7
Quiet Courage

Trail Truth: You can cry about it or laugh about it. Either way, you still have to keep going.

After finishing fifty miles, something inside me settled differently. I didn't hope I could do hard things anymore. I knew I could. Eventually, I found myself pointing that curiosity toward the idea of going a little farther.

That's how I ended up at the start of the Weymouth Woods 100K, a four-mile loop through the Sandhills Nature Preserve in Southern Pines, NC. The course looks pleasant enough until you spend hours on it. It's quiet. It's piney. It's peaceful in a way that feels kind at first, and then it quietly begins chewing you up. The sand slowly steals your legs. The trail rolls enough to wear you down. And the roots are everywhere. They even spray-painted some of the worst neon orange, which was thoughtful. Of course, that would be the very one I managed to trip over in my best Superman impression. Oof, if ever there was a time to question your life choices, this would have been it.

At some point the race tipped from hard to stupid-hard, especially after so many hours. You could either cry about it or laugh at it. There was a little aid station halfway around the loop run by two good ol' boys who, at first glance, looked like they'd be more at home in a deer stand than supporting runners. Turns out they were seasoned ultra veterans. Only in North Carolina do you get trail expertise, sarcasm, and Southern hospitality served together in the middle of the woods.

At one point I came in exhausted and over it and asked them, completely sincerely, "Do you have anything for a severe case of don't-give-a-shit-itis?" They didn't even blink. Buttered grits. Salt. Pepper. Handed to me like a medical prescription. And do you know what? It helped. Every loop after that, those guys had my grits waiting.

I don't even like grits.

Even with the humor, that course wears on you in ways you don't quite expect. It's a slow stacking of fatigue, loop after loop, hour after hour, steady accumulation until everything in you starts to sag a little.

By mile fifty, I finally stopped long enough at the main aid station to feel everything at once - the cold, the stiffness, and the weight of all the miles still ahead. That's when the tears came. The tired kind that says, *this is a lot, and I don't know how I'm going to keep going back out there.*

It's hard to describe the despair that settles in when you realize you still have hours left to run in the cold - and quitting isn't on the table. I needed that 100K finish. I wanted proof I was ready to take on the hundred.

This is where Darryl deserves serious credit. He took one look at me and recognized something deeply familiar to a man who's been married long enough. Exhaustion was obvious. The real issue was brewing underneath.

I was hangry.

There is a fine, sacred line between "emotional runner" and "woman who desperately needs a Snickers before someone gets hurt," and Darryl knows when I have reached it. He sprinted back to the aid station and returned armed with food like a man who values both his wife and his personal safety.

And here's the truth. It helped. It was enough to steady me, take a breath, and go back out.

Sometimes courage looks fierce. Sometimes it looks like a Snickers.

Those last miles were ugly. They were stubborn. Every loop was a negotiation. My brain had a lot to say and my body had opinions. There was cussing involved. My feet kept moving anyway.

Sometime around three in the morning, I finished in the quiet of the night. A kind volunteer practically carried me to the car when my legs decided they were completely done. I could never repay her for that simple, kind gesture.

And I need to tell the truth about how I felt afterward, because this matters.

That race was supposed to build my confidence. It didn't. I didn't walk away feeling ready for one hundred miles. I walked away humbled, shaken, and very aware of reality.

I remember thinking, good grief, that was spectacularly awful. How in the world am I supposed to go thirty-nine more miles than that someday?

That race didn't hand me certainty. It handed me a cold dose of reality.

Around this time, Darryl had left one of his drop bags behind from a prior running at Umstead. The associate race director offered to let us pick it up at her house. I thought I was just retrieving a bag.

I walked up to the porch, knocked, and Rhonda Hampton opened the door. I didn't realize what a pivotal moment this was. We still talk about it to this day.

Rhonda is known as an encourager for a reason. Her support comes without hype or pressure. There's this grounded, steady presence about her that softens fear the moment she looks at you. Her smile carries quiet confidence. When she listens, it's with her whole attention. Hard things feel possible in her presence, without ever pretending they aren't hard. The way she believes in people gently makes them believe in themselves a little more.

And that day, she did exactly that for me.
She gave me steadiness. Running at night was something to respect, she told me, and maybe even grow to appreciate. The course would teach me what I needed to know. The unknown doesn't automatically mean danger. Sometimes it simply means growth.

Her encouragement was calm, grounded, and unshakable. Rhonda helped me learn not to fear the dark or let my imagination spiral at every sound. And the snakes? I had a huge, irrational fear of them. But she helped me understand that we could share the trail. They didn't want to mess with me any more than I wanted to mess with them. We could coexist. That shift - from terror to respect - changed everything about how I moved through the woods.

Then she said something that didn't quite compute at the time: "If you can run 13.1, you can run a marathon. If you can run 26.2, you can do 50. If you can run 50, you can run 100." It didn't make sense to my brain, but I knew Rhonda was speaking from experience. It was one of those things you must see for yourself to believe.

And maybe the biggest thing she helped me see was this: Ultrarunning is a metaphor for life. It's about knowing when to push, when to rest, when to reset, when to ask for help, and when to keep going, gently, steadily, bravely.

Standing on her porch, I left feeling settled and steadier inside myself. The 100-mile dream didn't feel easy. It just didn't feel impossible anymore.

That shift changed everything.

Reflection Pause

When have I done something hard and walked away with more questions than confidence, and what did those questions teach me?

____

____

____

Where have I mistaken exhaustion or doubt for failure, when they were part of growing stronger?

____

____

____

Who in my life brings steadiness when things feel overwhelming, and have I acknowledged what a gift that is?

____

____

____

CHAPTER 8
The Reckoning Belongs to the Runner

Trail Truth: You don't sign up to prove you're tough. You sign up to meet yourself.

Umstead 100 Mile Endurance Run April 2012
William B. Umstead State Park, Raleigh, North Carolina

There are decisions in life that don't feel like events as much as thresholds. You can almost feel the line under your feet - the space between who you've been and who you're about to meet. Saying yes to one hundred miles was one of those moments for me. It felt like stepping toward something I needed to know about myself.

So, at forty-nine years old - an average woman with an average life in a very un-average moment - I stood on the starting line.

Umstead 100 is an eight-loop course, each loop 12.5 miles. On paper, that sounds tidy and manageable. Logical, even. Loop courses are tricky, though. Each one asks a slightly different question of you, and each one peels back another layer.

The first few loops did exactly what I hoped they would. They were steady. My legs did their job. My spirit stayed present. I ate, drank, listened to my body, and let the day unfold instead of trying to control it. I was tired in the expected ways, sore in the reasonable ways, and deeply grateful to still be moving.

By the time I passed fifty miles and the last of the daylight began to fade, the race shifted in a way only a hundred-miler can. The folks who stopped at fifty were done for the day, some by choice, some by necessity. They were getting warm, fed, and heading home.

Meanwhile, those of us still out there did what hundred-mile runners do.

We kept going.

That's when things get real.

The park grows quieter. The energy softens. The chatter fades, and what's left is something honest and raw. Now it's just the hundred-milers. Now it's you, your headlamp, your tired legs, and that small, stubborn voice inside saying, *Okay. This is where we find out what you're made of.*

They say you run the first fifty with your legs and the second fifty with your head. I didn't fully understand that yet, but I was about to.

Deep in the night, a thunderstorm rolled in out of nowhere. One minute it was dark and quiet, the next minute the trees were thrashing and the rain was coming at me sideways. My headlamp was basically a useless light bouncing off a wall of water.

Somewhere in that chaos, I ducked into a porta potty. When I came back out, my pacers were gone - swallowed up by the storm and confusion. Communication is rarely perfect at two in the morning, especially in a thunderstorm.

I was alone in the noise and dark, scared and angry. I'd trained for a lot of conditions, but not this. And I was worried about Darryl, somewhere out there running his own hundred-miler.

Then Bill Gentry showed up.

Bill is a seasoned ultrarunner from Virginia with an unmistakable Southern twang, calm and capable with a no-nonsense approach to problem-solving. He took one look at the situation and immediately understood what had happened.

Here's the part that still gets me: in the middle of his own 100-miler, Bill ran backward and about a mile out of his way to help me. In a thunderstorm. In the dark. Like it was the most obvious thing in the world.

He got everyone reunited, expectations reset, and the whole situation snapped back into order. Bill was a gift that night.

I was soaked and rattled, but no longer alone. We regrouped and carried on. That loop became the rain loop.

And yes, I finished it.

When it ended, I headed straight into race headquarters and changed clothes from head to toe. Socks. Shoes. Layers. Every soaked thing came off. It might have been the smartest decision I made all race. There is something profoundly settling about getting warm and dry before heading back into the dark. It doesn't erase exhaustion, but it makes you feel like yourself again.

I didn't call it self-care back then. I just knew I couldn't keep going if I stayed cold and soaked. I did the next small thing that would help me last.

I didn't know it at the time, but that simple act of taking care of myself so I could keep going would become essential later. When the miles weren't on a trail and there were no aid stations. When I was caregiving through my father's decline, running on empty, forgetting to eat, ignoring my own needs because someone else's felt more urgent.

Caregiving has its own version of endurance. The same rules apply: do the next small thing that keeps you standing. Change your clothes. Eat something. Rest when you can. Ask for help. You can't keep going if you stay cold and soaked - not in an ultra, and not in life.

Ultrarunning taught me that lesson on the trail. Caregiving forced me to remember it when it mattered most.

But that night, I didn't know any of that yet. The storm passed as quickly as it came, and a quieter kind of night settled in.

The kind where it's just you, the trail, your headlamp, your breath, and your thoughts. You don't get to hide from yourself in those hours. You keep choosing, step after step, to stay with yourself instead of quitting on yourself.

Eventually the darkness softened. The sky began to shift. Color returned to the world and a new day arrived.

There is nothing like sunrise in a hundred-miler. The dawning of a new day gives you perspective and enough hope to whisper, *You're still here. Keep going.*

For a while, that carried me.

Until it didn't.

There's an ultrarunning saying: whatever you're feeling now will change. It's true. One minute it's rainbows and unicorns. Five minutes later it's dog turds and trolls.

My turn came at mile ninety.

That's where the wheels came off.

Everything I'd been holding together stopped feeling hold-together-able. Pain flooded in. Every step felt like I was walking on shards of glass. My emotions spilled over whether I wanted them to or not.

And then the clock got loud.

Here's the truth: the trail may not care. The weather may not care. Your emotions may not care.

The clock absolutely does.

Cutoffs are real. Math is real. And when you're deep enough into a hundred, the margin between finishing and losing it all gets painfully thin.

I didn't know it then, but later I learned something that still brings tears to my eyes. Up near the finish line, my husband, who had already finished his own hundred, was waiting for me. He was exhausted but wouldn't rest until he saw me cross the finish line.

Darryl, always steady and grounded, the one who's rarely shaken, was openly sobbing and he didn't care who saw him.

Not because he didn't believe in me, but because he understood the math in a way I didn't yet and could see how narrow the path had become.

He would have taken every painful step for me if he could.

But that's the thing about a hundred-miler.

The reckoning belongs to the runner.

No one can run those miles for you.

And the truth is, by then I didn't even have the mental capacity to understand how close I was to not finishing in time. Exhaustion takes that from you. It narrows your world until there's no big picture, just the next step, the next breath, the next small decision.

So I did the only thing I knew to do.

I kept moving.

Not gracefully by any means, just shuffling along doing what I had to do.

And then finally, that last stretch appeared, the uphill finish at Umstead where your whole life seems to funnel into one strip of trail. Something inside me shifted. The fear loosened. The pain quieted. What remained was love, relief, disbelief, gratitude… and a strength I didn't fully know I possessed.

I did not walk that last hill.

After nearly thirty hours, through storm and separation, night and fear, getting lost and getting found, mile-ninety heartbreak, and every version of myself along the way… I ran.

I crossed that finish line in 29:39, with twenty-one minutes to spare in a 30-hour time limit. Let that sink in. After thirty hours of fighting for every step, I had about twenty minutes between "finisher" and "did not finish." I went straight into Darryl's arms and received my finisher's pendant.

I still wear it when life asks me to do hard things. I put it on, rub it for good luck, and remind myself, "Heck yeah. I can do this."

Reflection Pause

Where have I already lived my own "mile ninety," the place where everything felt fragile, but I kept going anyway?

___

___

___

Who has stood on the sidelines of my life loving me fiercely, even when they couldn't carry the miles for me?

___

___

___

Where have I underestimated my strength because I only remember the tears, not the courage it took to keep moving?

___

___

___

What current challenge in my life might not be asking me to be perfect, but simply to stay with myself and keep going?

___

___

___

What would it change if I truly believed: The reckoning belongs to me - and I can handle it?

___

___

___

CHAPTER 9
When the High Wore Off

Trail Truth: The finish line doesn't fix your life. It just shows you what you're capable of.

Finishing one hundred miles should have felt like the finish line to everything. It should have wrapped the story up with a satisfying bow and a sweeping "look what I did" moment. You'd think something that massive would settle comfortably into your DNA and carry you forward on confidence forever.

Instead, it dropped me into something far quieter, and in many ways, far harder.

There is a strange stillness that follows something monumental. For a while, I was riding that post-race high. I walked around with strength stitched into my bones, wearing resilience like a second skin. I had faced the storm, survived the dark, stared mile ninety in the eye, and come out the other side. For a stretch of time, I felt like I could do anything.

Then life nudged me and reminded me that growth is never a straight upward line.

Training started to fall apart, slipping away in small, sneaky ways. My body stopped bouncing back the way it used to. Runs that once felt like home started requiring more negotiating. I was tired more often than I wanted to admit. I was suffering from runner burnout.

And before I go any farther, I need to back up for a minute - because this part didn't happen after my first 100-miler. It happened before. I'd already run plenty of road races. I'd already fallen in love with trail running - the gritty, quiet kind where nobody cares what you look like and everybody's just trying to stay upright. If you run trails long enough, you fall. A lot. It's not a matter of if. It's when - and how bad.

My when happened early in a 25K at mile four, at a stream crossing. I went down hard and seriously hurt my shoulder. Race day adrenaline is a powerful thing, though. I dismissed the pain for the time being and kept running. That fall marked the beginning of a shoulder nightmare that lasted years.

The first surgery on my left shoulder in 2009 was brutal. It was honestly probably the most physical pain I've ever experienced. The kind that steals your sleep and turns time into thick sludge. They sent me home with serious pain meds along with sleep aids that left me in a fog I couldn't shake.

I hallucinated and barely knew what day it was. I wasn't myself.
The girls were in middle school at the time, and Darryl had to pick up all the slack I usually carried. He managed work, the household, the girls' schedules, and me - a wife who could barely function. The girls had to step up too, preparing meals and taking care of their own needs as best they could. We all pulled together to get through it, but the guilt of not being able to show up for my family the way I always had sat heavy on my chest.

Physical therapy was long, painful, and tedious. I pushed through it because that's what you do. You show up, do the work, and trust the process. Except the process wasn't working.

I'll never forget that appointment. My physical therapist looked at me, and I knew before he said a word. This wasn't going the way we'd hoped. He told me it was time to go back to the doctor, because my shoulder simply wasn't progressing the way it should.

The orthopedic surgeon confirmed it. I was one of those rare cases where the repair didn't hold. The shoulder hadn't knitted back together the way he'd hoped.

The despair I felt in that moment is hard to describe.

The idea of going through it all again, the pain, the rehab, the godawful cocktail of meds that turned me into someone I didn't recognize felt unbearable. But I had no choice. My body wasn't going to fix itself, and I couldn't live the rest of my life with a shoulder that didn't work.

So, I went back under the knife. I think it was about nine months later, though honestly, that whole period is a blur.

Thankfully, the second surgery had a better result. And I learned something I didn't expect: you can withstand a whole lot more than you think you can.

I was fortunate that I didn't get swept under into painkiller addiction. I hated the way they made feel foggy, disconnected, and not myself, so I took whatever bare minimum I could to manage the pain. It wasn't easy, but I was terrified of losing myself to those pills.

Eventually, the fog lifted. Slowly, very slowly, I started coming back.

And I'm telling you all of this because it matters later. It's part of what shaped me into the runner who eventually showed up at the start line of a 100-miler. It taught me what it feels like to start over - long before I ever tried to run one hundred miles.

Then, years later - after my second Umstead 100-miler - I needed surgery on my right shoulder. By then, I thought I knew what to expect. I'd been through this twice. I could handle it.

Except this time came with complications.

We had just gotten home from the hospital, and I was lying down, trying to rest, when Darryl looked at me with concern and said, "Hon, are you okay? You look like you're sweating."

I wasn't hot. That's when we realized the pain medication wasn't going into my body, it was leaking all over me. The pain port hadn't been inserted properly.

We called the doctor. They said, "Yep, you need to come back."

I remember being prepped for surgery again, and the medical staff debating over me lying there on the gurney whether to put me back under or not. I looked at them and said, I get a vote, this is non-negotiable. There was no way I was going to watch them operate on me while they reinserted that port. Thankfully, they agreed and put me under.

And then, about a week later, I was lying on the couch when I suddenly had the sensation that I couldn't catch my breath.

It came on quickly. I could barely raise my voice to get Darryl's attention. I knew something was wrong. I thought somehow I had a collapsed lung, though I couldn't imagine how that could be.

By the time we got to the ER, Darryl dropped me at the entrance, and I walked in to check myself in. By that point, my voice was barely a whisper. The fear I felt was palpable. I thought, *Holy crap, I'm in serious trouble here.*

They grabbed a wheelchair and whisked me straight back. Diagnosis: pneumonia. Because, as explained to me by the doctor, ultrarunners tend to have more efficient respiratory systems. While this works great for running, it can become a liability during post-surgical recovery. The irony is that the very adaptation that made me an endurance athlete - breathing efficiency - worked against me during recovery.

It seemed like I couldn't catch a break.

You try to stay upbeat through these setbacks, but I wasn't used to being someone who laid around. I've never been that person. And now I had no choice.

Three surgeries, recoveries, rounds of physical therapy, and versions of me learning the same lesson the hard way: you can't muscle your way through everything.

Obviously, I was completely out of commission for running. Each time I tried to come back, it was frustrating and humbling and maddening. It's not exactly starting at square one, but sometimes it sure feels that way.

Eventually, the fog of all that lifted and I delighted in the fact that I could walk to the mailbox. Then down the block, and then a mile.

The human body is an amazing machine. With a little time and a lot of patience, my body allowed me to run again. Nowhere near as fast or as far, but I was moving again.

But I also learned something else I didn't want to learn, but I did.

You can always start over again. You start from where you are, with what you have, and you build from there. Sometimes that means slower. Sometimes it means different. And sometimes it means redefining what "strong" even means.

Reflection Pause

Where in my life have I had to start over, and what did that teach me about my own resilience?

___

___

___

When setbacks stacked up, how did I keep going? What helped me stay tethered to hope?

___

___

___

Where have I been too hard on myself for not "bouncing back" the way I expected?

___

___

___

What small victory can I celebrate today, even if it looks nothing like what I once could do?

___

___

___

CHAPTER 10
Back to the Trail

Trail Truth: Volunteering wasn't a consolation prize. It was a way back to myself.

Starting over sounds brave when you say it out loud. In real life, it usually looks like sitting still long enough to feel what you've been avoiding and then figuring out how to live from there.

There is a particular kind of grief that settles in when your spirit remembers exactly what your body once did so freely, and your body simply can't meet it there anymore. I wasn't starting at square one - I had years of experience, mental toughness, knowledge. But my body had changed. Struggling through a single mile when I used to run them without thinking? That kind of humbling takes your breath away.

While all that was happening, life didn't hit pause so I could recover gracefully. There were still responsibilities. Caregiving, schedules, people needing things, and real life moving at full speed. Only now I was doing it with pain, limited mobility, and a body that suddenly felt suspiciously unreliable.

As I started getting lost in that cycle of burnout, injuries, and trying to claw my way back, I looked for meaningful ways to stay connected to the ultra-world without forcing my body to be something it couldn't be right then. That's when volunteering became more than "helping out." It became my way of staying rooted.

I have volunteered at Umstead for fifteen years now and so has my whole family. It's woven into the fabric of who we are.

We've all served in different ways over the years. Marissa used her graphic design skills to create T-shirts and paced runners - including her dad through multiple hundred-milers. Emmie worked the merchandise store and the aid station. Darryl and I both paced as well. But Darryl's favorite role is running the courier through the night, shuttling runners back from Aid Station 2 to headquarters - the ones whose day didn't end the way they hoped. He gets them warm and offers the kind of steady encouragement that doesn't feel like hype. More like, *Okay, this one didn't go your way, but you're not done. Try again when you're ready.*

Watching him do that reminded me that the heart of this sport isn't the finish line. It's the way people keep showing up for each other, year after year, especially when it's hard.

We're part of the Umstead 100 family. It's the same cast of characters who come back every year, steady and hilarious and big-hearted. They show up in the dark with headlamps and coffee and zero judgment. They've seen you at your best and worst. They cheer like it's personal, because to them, it is.

That kind of belonging matters when your identity starts wobbling.

And if you ever need inspiration or want to witness the strength of the human spirit, do yourself a favor: spend some time at the Umstead finish line on Sunday morning before the cutoff. Best seat in the house. There's never a dry eye in sight.

When my running season got shaky, staying connected to that volunteer family kept me from feeling like I had lost myself completely.

Following a year of stops and starts, 2017 became the year I threw my hat back in the ring. It's a natural instinct: when we lose our footing, we return to the places where we last felt like ourselves. Looking back, I still question why I signed up for Weymouth Woods. I knew what that course could dish out, yet I went anyway, perhaps searching for a spark of my former self, or perhaps proving I was a glutton for punishment. My training had been erratic, leaving me to rely on the hope that muscle memory and a little race-day magic would be enough to carry me across the line.

Not surprisingly, it didn't.

Early on, something inside me went quiet in a way I couldn't ignore. My body was moving, but my spirit wasn't with it. By the time I reached the 50K mark, I looked toward the trail ahead and I knew, deeply, calmly, and honestly that I was done. Not because I couldn't continue, but because I didn't want to.

That scared me more than pain ever had.

There was no meltdown, just a still, steady truth: this isn't my day.

DNF. Did Not Finish.

People love tidy redemption stories. They don't love DNFs. But here's what I learned the hard way. Sometimes the bravest thing a woman can do is stop pushing. Strength is knowing when compassion needs to replace grit. Sometimes walking off a course is not weakness but the wise choice.

Another pearl of wisdom from Sally comes to mind. Her take on a DNF is this: "a bad run is really a good run because you learn far more from your failures than your successes."

That DNF didn't break me. It humbled and softened me. It invited me back to movement without an agenda. I stopped chasing numbers and trying to "get back to who I was." I started walking and running because I needed air, trees, quiet, laughter, and space. The trails stopped being a proving ground and became a sanctuary again.

Healing doesn't always roar. Sometimes it whispers, *Take your time. I'm not going anywhere.*

Slowly, very slowly, something inside me lit up again. A gentle fire, steady and kind.

Reflection Pause

Where in my life has progress looked like a pause instead of a leap forward?

____

____

____

What part of me have I been trying to force, instead of listening to what I need?

____

____

____

When I can’t do what I used to do, how can I stay connected to what I love in a new way?

____

____

____

What is one small sign that something in me is beginning to light up again?

____

____

____

CHAPTER 11
When the Whisper Calls You Back

Trail Truth: Sometimes the whisper isn't calling you forward. It's calling you back to yourself.

Eventually, the idea of coming back to where it all started called to me again. Umstead, this time as a fifty-one-year-old woman. I'd logged so many miles there over the years that it felt like a comfortable warm blanket, familiar, like I belonged there. This was where a comeback made sense. Rhonda offered her gentle encouragement, like she always does, and assured me that with steady progress I could once again answer the call of the 100-miler.

The first time I showed up full of fear and adrenaline, wide-eyed and unsure of what I'd signed up for. This time the call sounded different. It felt quieter, more personal, like something I already knew in my bones.

I still had something to prove. I needed to know the first hundred wasn't a fluke, that I hadn't just caught lightning once and would spend the rest of my life talking about it like it was the only brave thing I ever did.

People warned me the second hundred might be harder. They were right. You can't unknow what a hundred miles takes. The bliss of ignorance is gone. There's no such thing as an easy hundred-miler, but at least the first time you don't know any better.

This time, I trained differently. Most of my training was with Jeannie and Rhonda, and because we live close enough to the park, we trained on the course itself. We ran loop after loop, week after week, until we knew every hill, every root, every bump, and every stretch of gravel that looks forgiving right up until you've been on it long enough.

Jeannie and I made an agreement early on for race day: run your own race. Two people don't stay together for a hundred miles, and neither of us wanted that kind of pressure hanging over us. We knew we'd be pulling for each other no matter where we were on the course, even if we weren't side by side. During training, there was one stretch that always caught my attention: Sawtooth 79. It's the hilly section on the back half of the course, around miles seven through nine on North Turkey Creek. It doesn't matter who you are, those hills are a beast. I had my own name for it too; one I won't repeat in polite company. Let's just say its initials were M.F. Hill, and every time I encountered it, I addressed it by name.

I decided on a small ritual for race day, something to anchor me when that section showed up again and again and again.

I carried eight rocks in my vest. Every time I crested that hill, I dropped one and said, "Up and over." That was it, a small promise I could keep. I wasn't thinking about one hundred miles. I was thinking about the next hill, the next climb, the next thing right in front of me.

Without planning it, Jeannie and I stayed side by side for the first fifty miles. It wasn't strategy, it just happened. We talked when we felt like it and went quiet when we didn't. It was the kind of steady that doesn't cost you extra energy.

Darryl crewed me again, and he was pure precision, like a pit crew at the Indy 500. I'd come in and he already had what I needed in his hands. Bottle swap. Food. Salt. Layers. An update on time elapsed because, you know, ultra math. Then off you go.

In my infinite wisdom, I'd set up my little mini aid station right next to the runners' bathroom for convenience. That turned out to be a constant assault on the senses for poor Darryl, and he deserves extra credit for enduring that without complaint.

The race did what races do. The miles stacked up. The easy parts stopped being easy, and my feet got loud. My brain started offering helpful suggestions like, you've done enough. You've proved your point. Let's go sit down forever.

Then the night came, and this time I didn't dread it the way I once did.

There's a strange peacefulness to running through the dark after you've been moving for hours on end. Your headlamp cuts a small circle through the trees, and the world shrinks down to dirt, breath, and the steady shuffle of shoes. Everything outside that beam stops mattering, and what's left is simple.

At some point, I stopped thinking in sentences and started thinking in commands.

Pick 'em up. Put 'em down.
Don't think. Just move.

It worked. The night became its own quiet place.

Somewhere in the later miles, one of my pacers showed up with a very specific mission: I was not hitting the wall on her watch.

She came armed with 80s music and attitude. She blasted it, looked at me like she meant business, and announced we were going to "prancercise" up a hill.

Then we started singing too, full volume, terrible form, completely committed. Two giddy women out there like a couple of Dancing Queens, bouncing up a hill in the woods like we had lost our minds.

We laughed so hard we cried, the kind of laughing where you can't catch your breath and your shoulders shake, and for a minute you forget your feet entirely. That was the point. She got me out of my head and back into motion, back into the moment, back into my body doing what it knew how to do.

The new day started to show up slowly, almost politely. The black turned to charcoal, charcoal turned to gray, and I realized I was still moving. That dawn felt like rebirth.

Darryl changed roles from pit crew to pacer, and he was steady, sure and locked in. He watched the math the way I couldn't anymore, and he kept it simple for me. He told me I wasn't chasing the cutoff this time, that I had built a comfortable margin. He told me I just needed to stay the course and keep on keeping on.

Then he said I was crushing it.

Crushing it.

And I remember thinking, seriously? Little ol' slow-ass me? Crushing it?

When the finish finally came into view, it felt deeply satisfying, the kind of satisfaction that settles into your chest and stays there. I came in nearly an hour faster, and I knew exactly why. I'd run it cleaner and smarter, with fewer mistakes and a lot less drama. By the end, everything hurt in the way it always hurts after a hundred miles, but none of that mattered. All I could think about was that I was still here, still moving, still doing the thing.

Then came the part I truly did not see coming.

At the turn into the final stretch, there was Emmie.
I didn't expect her to be there, and the second I saw her, it was like someone flipped a switch. Suddenly I felt like I was flying, like I had found an extra gear I didn't know I had.

We ran that last mile together, and then up the hill, and over the finish line. It was a runner's high like no other, the kind that makes you feel a little unhinged in the best way. If they could bottle it, I'd have a serious addiction.

Rhonda was there at the finish handing out buckles and pendants. When I came through and saw her, I felt it in my chest, like I'd made her proud. It was a full-circle moment for us, quiet and solid and real.

For me, it was simple. The race director shook my hand, and that quiet recognition said everything: you came back, you did the work, you finished.

I walked away from that finish line knowing something I hadn't known before. Finishing that second 100-miler left me with something solid: strength is a skill, and it can be practiced.

Running taught me how to work with what my body was telling me, instead of trying to override it. Over time I learned what helps, what backfires, what steadies me, and what happens when I keep showing up with a little patience.

If something in you has been nudging you while you read this, lean toward it. Follow the thread. Take one step and see what happens.

Reflection Pause

When have I quietly lost joy in something I once loved, and did I shame myself for it or offer compassion?

Where have I tied my worth to what my body used to do, and what would it feel like to untangle that?

When was the last time I honored a limit instead of bulldozing through it, and how did that protect me?

What have I come back from that once felt impossible, and have I truly acknowledged that strength?

CHAPTER 12
Where I Lost My Footing

Trail Truth: The hardest miles don't always happen on a trail.

I didn't know it yet, but the hardest miles of my life weren't waiting on a trail. They were waiting in ordinary rooms, in regular clothes, in the slow heartbreak of watching my father disappear in front of me. This is the part of the story where the finish lines stop being obvious.

We love the triumphant chapters. The comeback ones. The parts where strength shines bright and courage feels inspiring. What we don't talk about enough is the chapter where strength unravels. When the woman who once felt steady and capable suddenly looks in the mirror and barely recognizes herself. This is the stretch where resilience turns into simple survival, joy slips into numbness, and self-belief quietly erodes under the weight of everything piling onto your heart.

If I'm going to tell the truth in this book, and honor women in their full, real lives, then I have to tell this part too.

This was that chapter for me.

Here's what nobody tells you about midlife: it doesn't come at you one thing at a time. It comes all at once.

Around the time my father started slipping into dementia, my daughters were leaving for college. I was navigating menopause. And suddenly the role I'd held for eighteen years - hands-on mom - was shifting into something I didn't quite recognize.

I was still a mother. I would always be a mother. But mom-ing looked completely different now.

For nearly two decades, my identity had been built around being present, available, and needed. I knew their schedules, their friends, their worries. I packed lunches and signed permission slips and showed up at every event that mattered. My days were structured around their lives, and I was good at it. I was proud of it.

Then they left for college, and the house got quiet in a way that felt both relieving and gutting.

The worry never went away - it just changed shape. Now I worried from a distance. I had to learn to let them fly and trust their own judgment, even when every instinct in me wanted to fix things or protect them or remind them to make good choices. I had to remind myself, over and over, that this was what we wanted for them: independence, growth, and to live their own lives.

But that didn't make it any less disorienting.

At the same time, my father needed me in ways he never had before. My body was changing in ways I couldn't control. Menopause hit like a freight train. Sleep disappeared, emotions swung wildly, and my body stopped feeling like a familiar place to live inside.

I didn't have language for what I was feeling. I only knew I felt unmoored. Like I was standing in the middle of my own life and couldn't quite figure out where I fit anymore.

This is the perfect storm of midlife for so many women. Empty nest. Menopause. Aging parents. All of it hitting at the same time, each one asking something different from you, each one requiring you to let go of a version of yourself you thought you'd be forever.

And in the middle of all that, you're supposed to... keep going.

So, I did. Because that's what women do.

Looking back, I can see where it started: caregiving, something both sacred and devastating. My father was disappearing in slow motion. Every passing month I lost another piece of the man who raised me, loved me fiercely, and chose me when the world didn't expect him to. When your parent fades this way, you grieve in inches. You smile through a breaking heart. You hold everything together because love asks you to, and a little bit of you unravels each time.

What made it even more complicated was understanding the weight my father had already carried and for how long.

My father had been a caregiver for most of his later years, and really, long before that. When my parents divorced in 1970, he was granted primary custody, a rare outcome for a dad in that time and place. My grandmother, who moved in to help raise my brothers and me after the divorce, lived to be 102. My father cared for her for over thirty years. Try to imagine that. Thirty years. Then my stepmother suffered a debilitating stroke at 56, and my father cared for her until she passed at age 72. Sixteen more years of caregiving.

It was shortly after her passing that we started noticing Dad slipping mentally. At first, we chalked it up to exhaustion after so many years of caring for others, and the general forgetfulness that comes with getting older. But it became clear over time that this was more than just fatigue.

Dad was fiercely independent and did not want to be a burden to us, so we could not convince him to move in with us. He wanted to stay in his apartment where he had his social circle, his routines, his life. And even through dementia, Dad was a happy-go-lucky kind of guy. Everyone was his "best friend." He stayed active, walking the halls with his rollator and logging some serious distance. He enjoyed playing pool, breakfast with the men's group, and dancing. His friends and neighbors were patient and accepting of his worsening dementia. They looked out for him.

I was working part-time at this point, and it was a constant struggle to be there for everyone. I had always prided myself on being a hard worker and a reliable employee, but I couldn't be that person anymore when my day could be turned upside down with one phone call.

I took Dad to his numerous doctor appointments and had to delicately translate to the doctors when Dad would insist that he had Parkinson's - he did not - or other ailments his mind had created. At this point in my life, I felt like I wasn't good at anything. I gave the mandatory tasks a once-over and everything else kind of fell to the wayside. It felt like a merry-go-round I couldn't escape.

I came to dread my phone. Phone phobia is what I'd call it now. When it rang, my whole body would tense up. Shoulders to my ears, chest tight, that instant flood of dread about what wild ride this call might send me on. It could be nothing or it could be Dad fell and I needed to get to the ER. My body didn't wait to find out which one it was before reacting.

One day, Darryl came home from work and told me he had met a woman who was a Geriatric Care Manager, and he'd gotten her card. I had never heard of this before and didn't know what they did. Heather was a godsend. She assessed my father, sorted out all his medications and studied them for interactions with each other, took him to doctor appointments, and coordinated CNA care that we brought into his home. We found that it was more cost-effective to have caregivers come to him than to move him in assisted living. In addition, he didn't have to share a caregiver with numerous other people. The care was his, and his alone. We were blessed with some of the kindest most compassionate caregivers imaginable. They were truly angels walking on this earth.

Heather also taught me about the importance of cameras in the apartment not only to keep an eye on Dad, but to ensure that the caregivers were doing what they needed to do. It seemed a bit like an invasion of privacy, and I understand why some people would balk at the idea. But it gave me an immense sense of peace of mind to be able to check in on him, especially at night when worry kept me awake.

One of the other great blessings was the VA Aid and Attendance benefit. My father was an Air Force veteran, and we found that he was eligible for a monthly benefit to help cover the costs of ADLs - Assisted Daily Living. This took a huge financial burden off him and allowed him to stay in his apartment, as was his wish, until he passed.

Therapy, while yet another appointment to add to the schedule, was essential during this time. Dementia and end-of-life caregiving are a heavy weight. You need a safe space to let all the emotions you're feeling out without judgment. A place where you can say the things you're too ashamed to say anywhere else - like how tired you are, how angry you feel sometimes, how much you want it to be over so everyone can rest.

And then came the day I broke.

I was in my father's small apartment, counting out his pills for the week. I hadn't slept well in months. The thermostat was set to eighty because he was always cold, and I was sitting there sweating through my shirt, trying not to lose my mind. Dad had gone a little heavy on the Old Spice, and his country music was blaring - fine on a normal day, but when you're running on fumes it's simply too much.

It was sensory overload. And every time I tried to focus and get back to where I was, he interrupted me and I had to start over.

I could feel myself fraying in the slow, dangerous way exhaustion builds when it stacks up day after day. Finally, I snapped. I slammed the pill organizer down and said, "Dammit Dad, please. Just stop. Stop talking for one minute."

The words came out sharper than I meant. Sharper than he deserved.

Then I looked over and saw him crying.

That moment gutted me. It still does.

Because every caregiver I know has had some version of that breaking point - the moment where the weight is too much and the noise is too much and you think, *I can't do this anymore. I'm failing. I'm a terrible person.*

But the truth is, we are not terrible. We are human. We are tired. We are stretched beyond capacity, doing the best we can in a situation that asks more of us than any one person should have to give.

That day taught me something I didn't want to learn but needed: grace is not only something we offer others. It is something we have to offer ourselves.

And around that same time, quietly at first, my body started changing in ways I didn't recognize. It wasn't like menopause showed up on a single day and announced itself. It crept in while I was caregiving and grieving and running on fumes. My emotions ricocheted and my body stopped feeling like a familiar place to live inside.

And I didn't just "gain weight." I was coping.

I started overeating in small, private ways that felt harmless. The truth is, almost every time I left my dad's apartment, I treated myself to ice cream. I can't even tell you exactly why. It was comforting. It was predictable. It felt like the one small thing that was mine. And in the moment, it felt harmless.

Until it didn't.

The weight crept on silently, stacked on exhaustion, grief, emotional depletion, and survival.

This wasn't a few pounds from a stressful season. This was forty-five pounds of life on top of me. Forty-five pounds of heartbreak, caretaking, coping, and trying desperately to hold everything together while quietly falling apart myself.

And the truth is, this wasn't about weight gain.

I gave up on myself.

I remember outgrowing clothes I once loved. I donated them because I was certain those days were behind me. This was grief. Quiet, private grief over a woman I no longer believed would ever return.

The woman who once felt strong and alive now felt numb, exhausted, and deeply disconnected from herself. Food became comfort because I didn't have better words for what I was carrying.

I also started dreading the random run-ins, the kind where you bump into someone you haven't seen in a while, and you can feel your whole body tense. I was convinced they were thinking, *wow, she really let herself go*. Maybe they weren't thinking anything like that. But when you're already beating yourself up, you assume everyone else is too.

Even my favorite running store started to feel intimidating, which is ridiculous because they never treated me like anything but family. Still, walking in there made me feel like a fraud, like I didn't belong in that world anymore.

It wasn't them. It was my own head trash, loud and relentless, rewriting the story before anyone else could.

I avoided mirrors, photographs, and the places that once represented strength — because standing in them now only reminded me of everything I felt I no longer was.

During that season I wasn't running at all. My body and my spirit simply didn't have it in them. But I still found my way to the woods whenever I could. There's a spot by the lake, tucked far enough off the trail that no one wanders by, where I would sit and let myself fall apart. I'd pull my knees in, drop my head, and cry until the pressure inside me loosened enough to breathe again.

The woods have always been my sanctuary. Even when I couldn't run, I could still go there. Those trees never asked me to be strong.

They let me be.

Depression settled in quietly. I still functioned as best I could. I still showed up because that's what women do. We crumble privately, fix our mascara, and keep going.

Losing my father shattered my heart completely. Even when you know it's coming, it splits you open in ways nothing prepares you for.

And somewhere in all of that, something small but real flickered inside me. Just a whisper that felt like a hand on my shoulder: *You're still in here.*

I loved deeply. I survived more than people would ever know. My heart, though bruised and tired, still had tenderness left in it.

Healing didn't begin in my heart. I allowed myself to grieve without apology. I honored the love between a father and daughter. I forgave my body for coping the only way it knew how. I released the pressure to "bounce back" into worthiness.

Eventually, gently and slowly, and with a whole lot of grace, I started choosing myself again. I finally wanted to honor the person grief and life had shaped me into.

And honestly, that choice was braver than any finish line I've ever crossed.

I wasn't reclaiming the old me. I was discovering someone new.

Reflection Pause

Where have I carried shame that never actually belonged to me?

___

___

___

Where am I still grieving quietly without giving myself permission to feel it?

___

___

___

What have I quietly "given up on" because I stopped believing I was allowed to hope?

___

___

___

What would compassion toward myself look like, not someday, but today?

___

___

___

CHAPTER 13
A Different Kind of Ultra

Umstead Truth (Blake Norwood):

Eat before you are hungry, drink before you are thirsty, and walk before you are tired.

- Blake Norwood, Founder & Race Director, Umstead 100 Mile Endurance Run

Tradition: This is read aloud each year by the runner wearing bib #100.

Caregiving has a way of backing you into a corner. You keep showing up, because what else are you going to do. Then one day you realize you're running on fumes and calling it "fine."

When my father died, the noise finally quieted enough for me to understand what caregiving had been doing to me.

It's endurance with zero rules and a moving finish line. With dementia, you grieve while they're still here, and then you grieve again when they're gone.

For a long time, I thought I had to carry it all myself.

I can handle it.
I should be able to do this.
Everyone else needs me.
I'll be fine.

What I know now is simple. Doing the hard thing does not require doing it alone. Accepting help doesn't make you weak. It makes it possible to keep showing up with your whole heart.

When the calls stopped, I realized my nervous system had been living on high alert for so long it thought that was normal.

Reflection Pause

What kind of support would genuinely lighten my emotional, physical, or mental load?

___

___

___

Where am I grieving and what would it look like to honor that?

___

___

___

How can I begin to care for myself with the same devotion I've shown others?

___

___

___

If you're walking through caregiving, grief, dementia, or loving someone through decline, you deserve support.

The next pages are practical resources that helped me, plus a few I wish I'd found earlier. You'll also find the full resource section in the back of the book for easy reference.

CHAPTER 14
If You're Here Right Now When Grief Is Fresh

Trail Truth: There is no right way to grieve. There is only your way.

There may be women reading this book who aren't looking back on grief and exhaustion as a chapter they survived. You're living inside it right now. If that's you, I want to say this clearly: feeling weak, hollow, angry, numb, exhausted, or lost doesn't mean you're failing. It means you're a human being who has loved deeply and carried a lot.

A few reminders that matter when your brain is tired:

- You deserve help.
- You deserve rest.
- You deserve someone steady in your corner.

When I was in the thick of caregiving, losing my father, and running on high alert, I did get help, but I waited too long because I kept telling myself I could handle it. If you hear yourself saying that this page is here for you.

Grief Support:

GriefShare (free community-based grief groups nationwide)
griefshare.org This is a faith-based support group. Many local churches offer this program on an ongoing basis.

The Dougy Center (grief resources for adults and families)
dougy.org

National Hospice and Palliative Care Organization (grief resources)
nhpco.org

Megan Devine: Refuge in Grief (compassionate support, writing, and resources)
refugeingrief.com

Caregiver Support:

Alzheimer's Association 24/7 Helpline
1-800-272-3900
alz.org

Family Caregiver Alliance (education, support, online groups)
caregiver.org

AARP Caregiving Resource Center
aarp.org/caregiving

Therapy + Emotional Support:

Psychology Today Therapist Finder
psychologytoday.com

BetterHelp (online counseling)
betterhelp.com

Local hospice grief counselors
(many offer grief support even if your loved one was not in hospice)

If You Feel Overwhelmed or Unsafe:

If you are in immediate danger, call 911 (U.S.) or your local emergency number.

U.S. National Suicide & Crisis Lifeline: Dial 988

Crisis Text Line: Text HOME to 741741
If you are outside the U.S., many countries offer dedicated crisis lines and grief support networks. If you're not sure where to start, a local hospital, clinic, or community health line can help point you to the right resource.

If you need support, reach for it. Let someone help you carry a piece of this. You're worth that kind of care.

CHAPTER 15
The Net Underneath Me

Trail Truth: Sometimes the strongest thing you can do is let yourself be loved.

I used to think being strong meant handling things quietly and keeping the wheels on, no matter what. Turns out, strength has other forms too, and one of them is letting someone else step in and help carry the load.

Before I talk about the running family, the friends who have shared miles, tears, laughter, dirt, fear, ridiculous inside jokes, hope, and joy with me, I need to honor the man who has walked beside me through every part of this.

Darryl has been the rooted place when the world tilted. The calm when life spun too fast. The safe landing when I didn't know where my feet would touch down. In grief, he stood with me without trying to fix it. When I couldn't believe in myself, he believed for both of us. His hand held mine through doctor's offices and hospital rooms. When words came out messy and raw, and he listened. He celebrated who I am, more than what I achieved.

It's easy for that kind of presence to get overshadowed by the louder parts of a story. Medals, races, finish lines. The moments other people can point to. But the deepest strength in my life has come from someone whose love isn't loud. His support rarely shows up with fanfare. Instead, there's presence and patience. Steady care, over and over again. There's kindness in his eyes when I can't stand myself. When things get hard, he stays. I've never had to earn his love by being strong.

Darryl wasn't just there for me. He was there for my dad, too. They had a warm, close relationship, the kind you don't have to force. My dad adored him.

The night before my father passed, Darryl sat next to his bed. Dad wasn't conscious, but Darryl leaned in and said, "It's okay to let go. I'll take care of Linda."

I still believe my dad heard him.

That's the kind of man he is. When things got heavy, he didn't flinch or try to fix me. He simply stayed.

There are no medals for loving someone through their hardest seasons. If there were, he'd need a bigger shelf.

And even with a husband like that, I still needed more than one person. We all do.

I'm an introvert by nature, and when life gets heavy, my instinct is to cocoon. I go quiet. I tuck into the softest corners of my world. I try to hold everything together from inside my shell. It isn't avoidance. It's how I breathe. It's how I reset. It's how I survive.

My friends know this about me. They give me space when I need it - real space, the kind that feels like a blanket instead of abandonment. But they also know when to come find me. They know when the cocoon has stopped being rest and has started becoming isolation. They know when to knock gently on the door of my quiet and say, "Okay, friend, time to come back out now."

That kind of love is rare, and it has saved me more than once.

My running community became a different kind of lifeline. These friends have seen the unfiltered version of me - the tired, sweaty, laughing, crying, determined, doubting, joyful, stubborn, hopeful version. There is something honest about moving through hard miles beside someone. Pretenses fall away. Conversations get real. You share snacks, miles, frustrations, and little victories, and somehow that weaves people into your life differently.

They have been the people who check in when life goes quiet. The ones who understand what courage looks like long before a finish line. The ones who know when to challenge you, when to tell you to rest, and when to simply walk beside you without saying a word.

Community steadies you inside the pain, softens the sharpest edges of grief, and keeps you from being alone in it. And maybe the most healing gift of all is this: it gives you witnesses. People who can look at you and say, "I see you. I'm not going anywhere."

If you are reading this and you feel alone, hear me when I say this gently but firmly: you are not meant to carry your life alone. You deserve people who stand beside you when the load gets heavy. You deserve friendships that know when to turn back for you and walk with you instead of ahead of you. You deserve arms that feel safe and hearts that feel steady.

And if those people aren't in your life yet, do not believe it's too late. Life is still introducing you to people who will matter. There are still hearts meant to meet yours. There are still friendships waiting to be lived.

Strength is shared endurance, chosen togetherness, and the humble courage to allow yourself to be held. I am who I am today not because I endured, but because I was loved while I endured by my husband, who remains my steady ground; by friends who tightened the net underneath me when I started to fall; and by a community that refused to let me forget I belong.

I will be forever grateful.

Reflection Pause

Who are the people who have quietly stood with me in my hardest times? Have I truly acknowledged what their presence meant?

Where in my life have I tried to carry everything alone? What would it look like to let someone shoulder even a small corner of that weight?

When has someone turned back for me instead of walking ahead? How did that change how I saw myself, and how I understood love?

Have I ever believed I needed to "be strong" to be worthy of love or support? What would it feel like to loosen that expectation?

Where do I still long for connection, friendship, or community? If I took one brave step toward it, what might that step be?

____

____

____

How might I also be that person for someone else, steady, kind, present, without losing myself in the process?

____

____

____

CHAPTER 16
The Mercy of the Trail

Trail Truth: Presence often shows up long before strength does.

Being held by the people who loved me gave me enough steadiness to try again, and sometimes that's all a woman needs to begin.

Starting over can feel fragile. It feels like walking around with your skin turned inside out. It feels like trying to learn your own heart all over again and realizing you don't recognize the person carrying it.

After losing my father, after caregiving burnout and that quiet emotional collapse that sneaks up on you, after menopause reshaped my body and survival became my default setting, I found myself in a place I never expected. I was trying to come back to myself when I had lost track of who "myself" even was. I wanted to feel like I lived inside my own life again.

My first step back was the woods.

The woods have always been my sanctuary, the place where my breath finds me again. I went back to the trails the way you go back to something that once saved you. The woods don't ask questions. They just let you show up. They let you breathe, and when you've been holding your breath for a long time, that kind of relief matters more than people realize.

Those early walks were hard. Many days brought tears. Even so, they reminded me of something I had forgotten: some days, showing up was the win.

Then there was the part I couldn't ignore anymore. My knee wasn't "a little off." It was failing me.

The pain was constant. Sleep was garbage. Movement came with fear. My days started organizing themselves around avoiding pain instead of living. I kept hoping things would turn a corner, like my body would finally get the memo and cooperate. My knee had other plans. It wasn't going to fix itself, and I had to say that out loud before I could do anything about it.

Hearing the words knee replacement landed as more than medical. It landed in my identity. Movement had always been how I celebrated life, how I processed grief, how I steadied myself, how I found my way back when I got lost. The idea of the joint that carried me through storms and joy and grit being taken apart and rebuilt felt terrifying. I worried about aging and independence. I worried about what would happen if it didn't go well.

Living inside limitation and pain wasn't a life I could accept.
So, I chose the only way forward I had. I wasn't brave or fearless. I was out of options. On surgery day I felt scared and surrendered, quietly praying that something better waited on the other side.

Recovery humbled me, and yeah, it hurt.

It was swelling, ice packs, compression sleeves, and sleep that never did its job. Physical therapy was hard, frustrating and emotional. I had plenty of moments where I wanted to chuck the ice machine out the window. Progress showed up in inches.

And yes, inches still count.

I think of my friend Deb with real tenderness. We met at the greenway, and I walked one mile with my cane. Pretty damn humbling, and still, it was progress. She met me where I was and let me shuffle alongside her with quiet patience and steady companionship.

In time I graduated to slow walking without the cane. In those early weeks, it was hard to picture myself running trails or riding a bike again. Then one day you feel steadier. Another day you catch a glimpse of yourself again. Different, for sure, but still you.

There were tears. There were small triumphs that no one else would ever clap for. Wobbly steps. A day when pain didn't win the whole day. The strange relief of realizing movement was slowly turning into trust again.

Healing took real time. Strength returned the way embers return to a fire you thought had gone out.

When I finally made it back to the trails, I walked. But walking meant independence. It meant hope was back in the room. Out there, I learned something that changed the way I relate to my body: movement doesn't have to look strong to be strong. Slow counts. Gentle counts. Forward counts.

That slower season softened me. Respect showed up where pressure used to live. Gratitude moved in where proof used to sit. I stopped treating my body like a machine that should perform on command. I started treating it like something sacred, something that had carried me through a lot and deserved kindness now.

Over time, my spirit nudged me again. Challenge still had a place in my life.

That's when I found timed ultras, the kind where the goal isn't perfection or distance. The goal is being out there for a set number of hours. You go as far as your body and heart allow. You rest when you need to and keep moving when you can.

That format healed something tender in me. It reminded me that strength didn't disappear. It changed shape. It taught me that challenge can be loving. It showed me that beginning again doesn't make you weak. It means you still want something, and that you're alive enough to go after it.

What Really Changed

Somewhere in the middle of recovery, my relationship with my body changed. For a long time, I treated my body like a project. It needed to look a certain way. The scale needed to cooperate. There had to be proof that I was "doing it right." It was exhausting, and honestly, it made me miss the whole point.

Now I care a lot more about capability.

Feeling steady on a rocky trail. Climbing stairs without bargaining with my knees. Carrying my own suitcase and stepping into new places without that little voice whispering, careful now. Keeping saying yes to the things I love, whether that's a hike, a bike ride, a trip, or a random Tuesday where my nervous system needs the woods.

That's it. That's the whole speech.

Pilates has helped more than I ever expected. It builds the kind of strength that quietly shows up everywhere else. Core, balance, posture, stability. All of this matters when you're stepping over roots on a trail or moving around on tired legs.

These days, I'm not chasing some perfect version of fitness. I'm paying attention. I'm staying in the habit of movement because it keeps me feeling like myself.

I keep it simple, and I keep showing up.

I still like a challenge. I always will. I just want it to feel clean, like I'm doing it with my body instead of dragging it behind me.

Reflection Pause

Where in my life do I need permission to begin again, and can I offer that permission to myself instead of waiting for someone else to approve it?

____

____

____

Where have I convinced myself "I am done," when maybe the truth is simply "I am different now"?

____

____

____

What does gentle strength look like for me now, and how can I honor it instead of chasing who I used to be?

____

____

____

CHAPTER 17
Your One Wild and Precious Life

Trail Truth: Your one wild and precious life is happening right now.

I'm still figuring out what healing looks like.

It's quieter than I expected. It shows up as steady choices, practical habits, and the way you live your days when no one's watching.

When I signed up for my most recent timed ultra, I wanted to answer a question I'd been circling for a long time. I set it up in a way that gave me nowhere to hide. I went on my own without my familiar safety net. Just me, my choices, and the question that kept tapping me on the shoulder.

Could I take care of myself?

My friend Deb has run a marathon on every continent, including Antarctica. I remember thinking, okay, Linda. If she can go to Antarctica, you can go to Emerald Isle by yourself.

This race was about trusting myself. Could I fuel for hours without turning it into a battle? Could I manage fatigue? Could I stay steady when doubt showed up and started running its mouth?

I believed I could, and that belief mattered.

So, I moved for hours. I ran when it made sense and power-walked when it didn't. I paid attention to what I needed and handled it like it mattered. Calm turned out to be a skill, and I practiced it on purpose. I wasn't chasing misery for bragging rights. I worked with myself through the effort, one decision at a time.

The race was The Tidelands 24, held in the Croatan National Forest. It's a soft dirt loop tracing marshland near Emerald Isle, North Carolina, and that day the world felt wide and alive. I watched the tide come in and go out like it had all the time in the world. The sunset was so stunning it brought tears to my eyes.

Low points still show up in ultras, and mine arrived right on schedule.

Rhonda and Angela texted me and said, "Eat a Snickers." So, I did. I grabbed an Almond Joy too, for insurance and for joy. I was out there solo, and my people still had me. Darryl checked in. My daughters checked in. Mia checked in too, the friend I met back in Couch-to-5K days when I was just getting started.

Later that afternoon, as I crossed the timing mat to start another loop, a woman called out, "I want to tell you, I've noticed you've been smiling all day."

That landed hard, in the best way. It was the clearest signal I could have asked for.

Somewhere along the way, I had found my way back to myself.

By the end, I'd covered forty-five miles. I finished tired and content, and I felt proud in a quiet, private way. No audience needed. The win was simple. I could take care of myself out there.

That race left me with a kind of confidence I hadn't felt in a while, and it followed me home.

Hiking met me differently after that. It asked for effort and gave me space. It brought me back to the simplest medicine I've always found on trails: quiet, fresh air, and the reminder that my body still belongs to me.

After a while, movement started to feel less like a pastime and more like something practical. Something reliable in real life. That's where Pilates came in.

I knew I needed it, and I knew it was going to humble me. It took me six months to work up the nerve to walk into the studio. With an artificial knee and two bum shoulders, my worry wasn't whether I'd like Pilates. My worry was failing at it in public. My brain served up the whole buffet: what if I can't do this, what if I look ridiculous, what if everyone else knows what they're doing and I'm the only one lost?

I walked in anyway.

That one decision did more than strengthen my core. It reminded me I'm allowed to start where I am. At this age, core strength and balance aren't vanity goals. They're life goals.

There's a sign on the wall in the studio that says, "Do Pilates. Do Life." Every time I see it, it reminds me why I'm there. I want to live well in the body I've got, and I want my body to support the life I still plan to live.

Travel started to feel possible in a new way too. It felt like a choice I could make again. Not an escape hatch, just a widening. More wonder, more perspective, more moments that wake you up to your own life.

I'm happiest in the in-between moments: wandering markets, sitting in quiet cafés, walking neighborhoods, hiking trails, blending into the mix while real life happens around me.

Somewhere along the way, something else got clearer too. My daughters were watching.

Those little girls who once bounced around ultramarathon aid stations handing out hugs, snacks, and joy grew into women who understand what real strength looks like. They've seen it up close, and it's imperfect and lived.

Marissa, once painfully shy, became a woman who lives boldly. She moved to Seattle, built a meaningful life, found work that feeds her creative spirit, spends weekends skiing and rock climbing, and runs marathons because it lives in her bones. Emmie earned her PhD in neuroscience and devoted her research to Alzheimer's and dementia, turning love and loss into purpose. She still runs too.

They are kind, brave and compassionate. They didn't get that because life spared them. They got it because they watched what it looks like to keep showing up.

I'm not claiming credit. I'm naming something we don't say out loud enough. Our kids see us. They notice whether we stay present inside our own lives. Without realizing it, my daughters inherited something more useful than advice.

They inherited permission.

Now I'm sixty-two, stitched together with scars, tenderness, humor, and more wisdom than I ever expected to earn. I'm still moving forward, still saying yes, because I want a life that feels honest and lived.

This is my one wild and precious life, and I intend to live it.
If there's a takeaway here, it's simple. Do more of what makes you feel alive while you can. Your life doesn't have to be impressive. It has to be lived.

Reflection Pause

What part of me is quietly asking to come back online, not someday, but now?

___

___

___

Where have I been waiting to feel "ready" before I let myself live, and what would one small yes look like this week?

___

___

___

What do I know about myself now that I didn't know before everything I've lived through?

___

___

___

CHAPTER 18
You Still Get a Next

Trail Truth: The hard seasons don't get the final word.

If there's one thing I want you to take from all of this, it's this: a next still exists.

Life can knock the wind out of you. It can keep piling things on until it feels like you're living with your shoulders up around your ears all day, every day. Then one afternoon you catch yourself laughing, real laughing, and it surprises you because you forgot your body even knew how to do that. Little moments like that matter. They don't fix everything, but they remind you there's still room.

Most of the time, the way forward doesn't arrive as a big decision. It's the smaller stuff that adds up. Eating before you're running on fumes. Sleeping when you can. Saying no without writing a full essay to justify it. Admitting what isn't working anymore. Taking a step that belongs to you, even if it's tiny.

Here's what I mean in plain language. Life is happening right now. It's okay to want more than getting through the day. It's okay to make room for plans and curiosity and laughter, even if things are still messy. It's okay to do something that scares you a little, as long as it's the kind of scare that makes you feel awake.

Nothing you've lived is useless. It's in you, whether you can name it yet or not.

If you're the kind of woman who takes care of everyone else first, try putting yourself back on the list. Talk to yourself like you talk to the people you love. Pay attention to what your body has been asking for. When rest is the right call, take it without turning it into a character flaw.

And when you forget, come back to the simplest truth in the room.

A next still exists.

Reflection Pause

Who did you used to be, and who are you now?
Without judgment, who were you before loss, before change, before this stretch of life? What parts of you have softened? Strengthened? Returned? Arrived for the first time?

____

____

____

What does strength look like for you today - not years ago, not compared to anyone else, but right now?
Does strength look like rest? Boundaries? Asking for help? Starting over? Saying no? Saying yes?

____

____

____

What do you need to grieve that you haven't fully grieved yet?
Grief isn't only for death. We grieve dreams, identities, health, roles, seasons, and versions of ourselves. What deserves more tenderness than you've given it?

____

____

____

What are you allowed to release?
What expectations, timelines, guilt, perfectionism, or old stories no longer belong to you? What would it feel like to loosen your grip, even a little?

____

____

____

What would kindness look like right now?

If you spoke to yourself the way you'd speak to someone you love, what would you say? What would compassion look like in action?

____

____

____

What do you want to carry forward?

What wisdom do you want to keep close? What truths do you not want to forget when life gets loud again?

____

____

____

AFTERWARD

A Gentle Guide to Beginning: Where to Start

If you've made it this far, something in you is paying attention. That matters.

Pause for a second and take that seriously. Wanting something again is a real thing, especially after years of handling everything.

A lot of us spend years being the reliable one. The one who keeps the wheels on. Somewhere in there, it gets easy to forget you still get a vote in your own life.

Here's a simple way to start.

1) Find your why
Your why doesn't need to impress anyone. It needs to be true. It's the thing you come back to when you're tired, annoyed, busy, or questioning your life choices.

A few that tend to ring true in midlife:

- I want to feel like myself again.
- I want to feel steady in my own body.
- I want my energy back.
- I want something that's mine.
- I want to trust myself again.
- I want to feel capable in my everyday life.
- I want to stop negotiating with myself every day.

Write one sentence. Keep it somewhere you can see it. When things get rough, your why is the anchor, not the pep talk.

2) Pick your thing
For me, it was running. It asked honest questions, and it gave honest answers. It also cleared my head.

Your thing can be anything that pulls you forward a little: walking, hiking, lifting, Pilates, cycling, swimming, a class, a trip, a creative project, a new skill. Choose something that feels interesting enough to keep coming back to.

If it makes you slightly nervous and slightly excited, pay attention. That combination is usually a clue.

3) Make it doable
Start with a plan you'll follow on a normal week.

Two days a week is fine. Ten minutes counts. One class a week counts. This is not a personality makeover. It's a practice.

Consistency beats intensity and you'll feel that sooner than you think.

4) Expect real life to show up
There will be busy weeks. Low-energy days. Schedules that explode. That's part of it.

Decide ahead of time what you do when the plan gets wobbly. Keep a default: a shorter version, a walk instead of a workout, or ten minutes that gets you started.

The win is staying in the conversation with yourself.

5) Decide what counts
A lot of success happens in quiet places.

- The day you begin.
- The day you show up when it would be easier to skip.
- The first time you notice you feel steadier.
- The day you keep a promise to yourself, even a small one.

That's the kind of progress that changes a life.

Before you go

You don't need a perfect plan. You need a next step you'll actually take. Pick one why. Pick one thing. Start small. Then do it again next week.

Reflection Pause

What do I deeply want, even if I feel nervous to admit it?

___

___

___

Where have I underestimated my strength before?

___

___

___

If judgment disappeared for a moment, what would I begin?

___

___

___

How can I treat my body and my story with more tenderness?

___

___

___

READER SUPPORT

Grief Support Resources

Grief shows up in a lot of ways. Losing a person is one of them. Losing health, identity, roles, relationships, or the life you thought you were living can hit just as hard. Support helps.

Grief support (U.S.)

National Alliance for Grieving – education, community, and resources

- GriefShare – in-person and online grief support groups
- Modern Loss – community, stories, and practical resources
- What's Your Grief – articles, tools, and courses
- The Dougy Center – support for families and children navigating grief

Outside the U.S.

Try searching:

- "grief support" + your country
- "bereavement support services" + your city/region

Mental and Emotional Health Support

Getting support for your mind and nervous system counts as health care. Period.

Crisis support (U.S.)

- 988 Suicide & Crisis Lifeline – call or text 988 (24/7)
  Support for emotional distress, suicidal thoughts, or any moment you feel unsafe.
- Crisis Text Line – text HOME to 741741 (24/7)
  Free, confidential support via text.

Therapy directories

- PsychologyToday.com – therapist directory
- TherapyDen.com – inclusive, identity-aware directory
- Open Path Collective – reduced-fee therapy options

Outside the U.S.

Search:

- "mental health crisis line" + your country
- "therapy" + your location

Caregiver Support

If you are caring for someone who is ill, aging, or declining, the emotional toll is real and it stacks up fast.

- Family Caregiver Alliance – education, resources, support
- Caregiver Action Network – guidance, advocacy, community
- Local hospice programs and hospital caregiver services – many offer free support groups and counseling

Women, Midlife, and Emotional Well-Being

Midlife can be a full-body recalibration. Help exists for that too.

- North American Menopause Society (NAMS) – trusted menopause and midlife health information
- Midlife counseling and support groups – many therapists specialize in identity change, transitions, and grief

When You Need Help Right Now

If you feel overwhelmed, unsafe, or like you cannot carry what you're holding, reach out for immediate help.

In the U.S., call or text 988.

Outside the U.S., contact your local emergency number or search "crisis line" + your country.

If making the call feels like too much, ask someone you trust to sit with you and help you do it.

Letter to the Reader

Dear friend,

If you're closing this book feeling tender, quiet, or a little rattled in that way truth can do, I want to say something plainly. Life falling apart did not get the last word. You're still here, still breathing, still reading, and that matters.

Grief leaves fingerprints. Loss changes the furniture inside a person. Life has a way of rearranging us from the inside out, and it can take a while to recognize yourself again.

The only way through is forward and forward does not require speed. Some days it's one small, stubborn step. A step still counts.

If you're carrying pain that won't hurry up and leave, that's part of loving and losing. If you're taking your time, that's part of coming back to yourself. And if you're doing it quietly, without an audience, that still takes real courage.

Strength rarely looks impressive up close. Most of the time it looks like getting up and doing the next doable thing. It looks like staying present when checking out would be easier. It's choosing yourself when you're tired of being the strong one for everyone else.

If anything from these pages stays with you, let it be this. Building can start right where you are, inside the life you're living today. You get to begin from here.

I'm grateful you spent this time with me and let my story sit beside yours. Keep going in whatever way makes sense right now. Keep your sense of humor when you can. Give yourself more grace than you've been giving. Keep leaning toward what helps, even if it starts small and looks simple.

With care,

Linda

Appendix

Tools for Beginning Again
Practical pages to come back to when life gets loud.
How to Use This Appendix
These pages are here to support you. Start anywhere. Use what helps. Come back when you're ready. The goal is a steady next step, not a perfect plan.

Appendix A: A Quick-Start "Begin Again" Plan

The 10-Minute Rule
On the hardest days, give yourself ten minutes.
Walk for ten minutes. Stretch for ten minutes. Journal for ten minutes. Sit outside for ten minutes.
If you stop at ten minutes, it still counts. Ten minutes is how momentum gets rebuilt.

The 3-Day Reset
When everything feels off, try this for three days.
Day 1: Body

- Drink water like it's your job.
- Move for 10–20 minutes (a walk counts).
- Eat one real meal (protein + something colorful).

Day 2: Mind

- Reduce input (less news, less scrolling).
- Do one small task you've been avoiding.
- Get outside, even briefly.

Day 3: Heart

- Text or call one safe person.
- Do one kind thing for yourself without earning it.
- Go to bed like you matter.

The "If–Then" Plan (for bad days)

If I feel overwhelmed, then I will do one small thing for ten minutes and stop.

- If I feel ashamed, then I will name it and choose one next step anyway.
- If I feel alone, then I will reach out to one person, even if it's just a text.
- If I feel stuck, then I will go outside and walk until my nervous system settles.
- A note on progress: progress is layered. It builds the way endurance builds.

Appendix B: The Caregiving Ultra Toolkit

Caregiving is endurance work. It asks more than most people understand. If you're in it now, you deserve tools and support.

Signs More Support Would Help

Support would help if:

- You're exhausted most days, even after rest
- You feel on edge, numb, or irritable more than you feel like yourself
- Stress is living in your body (sleep issues, headaches, tension, panic)
- You've lost interest in things that usually steady you
- You're doing everything and still feel like you're underwater

Three Supports That Can Change Everything

- A geriatric care manager
- In-home caregivers
- Therapy

Questions to Ask Yourself (Often)

- What's mine to carry, and what can be shared?
- What would help me breathe again?
- If my best friend were living my life, what would I want for her?

Appendix C: Dementia and Grief Resources

Dementia Support + VA Support

National organizations and helplines:

- Alzheimer's Association: alz.org
- VA Caregiver Support Program: caregiver.va.gov

Books that helped:

- *Questions and Answers on Death and Dying – Elisabeth Kübler-Ross*
- *When Is Enough, Enough? – Teepa Snow*
- *Dementia Caregiver Guide – Teepa Snow*

Websites/Videos:

- National Institute on Aging (Alzheimer's resources)
- "An Act of Love: Talking with Your Family About Serious Illness and End of Life" (YouTube)
- VA Aid and Attendance benefits: va.gov

Grief Support Organizations:

- GriefShare: griefshare.org
- Transitions LifeCare: transitionslifecare.org

What to Search for Locally

- "caregiver support group dementia" + your city
- "Alzheimer's caregiver group" + your county
- "hospice grief counseling" + your area
- "family caregiver respite services" + your state

Small reminder: you get to be the daughter, the spouse, the human. Let experts help with the rest.

Appendix D: Scripts for Hard Conversations

Because when you're stressed, your brain becomes a bag of squirrels.

The "We Need Help" Conversation (Family)
"I can't keep doing this alone. I'm at my limit. I want a plan that includes real support. Here's what I need help with: ____. Can you take ____ and ____?"

The Boundary Script
"I love you. Here's what I can do: ____. Here's what I'm not available for anymore: ____. Here's what I need going forward: ____."

The Doctor Appointment Script
"I'm the caregiver. I need clarity. Can you explain what we're dealing with, what to expect next, and what support services you recommend? What should I watch for that means 'call immediately'?"

Questions for In-Home Care or Facilities

- What does a typical day look like?
- How do you handle agitation, wandering, or nighttime confusion?
- How do you communicate changes to family?
- What's included and what costs extra?
- What happens if my loved one declines quickly?

The "I Need a Break" Script
"I'm taking a break. I'll be back at ____. Here's what's covered while I'm gone: ____."

Appendix E: The "I Feel Like a Fraud" Page

For the running-store feeling. The "I don't belong here anymore" feeling.

A cleaner truth: people are living their own lives. Your mind is the one putting you on trial.

When Shame Shows Up, Answer It

- "I survived a hard stretch. I'm allowed to come back."
- "Belonging starts with showing up."
- "My brain is telling stories. I'm choosing the next step anyway."

A 60-Second Reset

Hand on your chest. Inhale slow. Exhale longer.
Say: "I'm safe. I'm allowed. I'm coming back."

Appendix F: A Movement Menu for Midlife Bodies

This is about keeping your body capable, steady, and yours.

Choose What Fits Right Now

- Low capacity day: 10-minute walk, gentle stretch, sit outside and breathe
- Medium capacity day: walk + light strength, Pilates, easy hike
- High capacity day: longer hike, timed-event training, strength session
-

Walking and Hiking Progression

- Weeks 1–2: 10–20 minutes, 3–4 days/week
- Weeks 3–4: 20–30 minutes, add one longer day
- Week 5+: add hills or trails once a week

Pilates (and the bravery of walking in the door)

If it took six months to work up the nerve, welcome to being human.
Core strength and balance are life goals.

Strength Priorities as We Age

- Core stability
- Balance
- Hips and glutes
- Mobility
- Fall prevention

Appendix G: Personal "Begin Again" Pages

(You can journal these, print them, or revisit them anytime.)

My Why (right now)

I want to begin again because:

____

____

____

Where I Am Right Now

Right now, life feels like:

____

____

____

What feels heavy:

____

____

____

What feels hopeful:

____

____

____

My Support List

People I can reach for:

____

____

____

Support I want to add:

____

____

____

My Next Tiny Step (48 hours)

One small step I can do within two days:

____

____

____

Boundaries I Need

What I'm no longer available for:

____

____

____

What I am choosing instead:

____

____

____

My Joy List (tiny counts)

Three things that still make me feel like me:

____

____

____

Acknowledgments

This book has my name on the cover, but it was never a solo effort. I've been carried, steadied, and loved in ways I'll never fully be able to repay. If you're in these pages, you mattered to the story, and you mattered to me.

Darryl, thank you for being the steady one, especially when I wasn't. Thank you for your patience when life got heavy, and for loving me in the middle of it, not just on the other side. Your kind of support is quiet, constant, and rare.

Marissa and Emmie, thank you for your humor, your kindness, and the way you bring light into my life. Thank you for letting me be both your mother and a woman still figuring things out. Watching you grow into who you are has changed me for the better, and I'm proud of you in ways I don't even have good words for.

To my friends, and to my running and walking family, thank you for being my people. Thank you for the miles, the check-ins, the inside jokes, the honest talks, and the way you showed up without needing me to explain everything. Whether we were running, powerwalking, shuffling, or doing the best we could on tired legs, your companionship mattered more than you know.

Dr. David Jones, thank you for your care and skill, and for understanding the kind of life I wanted to get back to. You helped give me back the ability to move through the world the way I love to.

Olivier Chassin, DPT, thank you for your patience, your expertise, and your steady guidance on the days progress felt slow. You helped me rebuild both strength and confidence, one step at a time.

To the women who shared their stories, trusted me with their truths, and kept showing up in their own lives, thank you. Your courage and honesty shaped this book more than you realize.

And to you, the reader, thank you for spending your time here. If you're grieving, rebuilding, starting over, or finding your footing again, I hope something in these pages makes you feel seen and less alone. I wrote this with you in mind.

About the Author

Linda Banks is a writer who loves the outdoors, travel, and any excuse to get into the woods. She wrote this book for the same reason she loves a good walk with friends: most things feel more manageable after fresh air, honest conversation, and a few steady steps forward. She lives in North Carolina with her husband, Darryl.

www.ingramcontent.com/pod-product-compliance
Lightning Source LLC
LaVergne TN
LVHW090527110826
845146LV00003B/1014